The Highly Sensitive Person and Career

Tracy Cooper, Ph.D.

Invictus Publishing, LLC

Thrive: The Highly Sensitive Person and Career

Invictus Publishing, LLC
2303 South 16th Street
Ozark, MO 65721
Author's web site: www.drtracycooper.wordpress.com

Printed in the United States of America
Published by Invictus Publishing, LLC
First printing: August 2015

Dedication

This book is dedicated to every highly sensitive person who has ever felt beaten, bruised, battered, ignored, or misunderstood in their quest to build a career in societies where they are neither understood nor valued. For every sweet soul who has climbed to the proverbial mountaintop, many more lie bloodied and beaten on the slopes. I dedicate this to who are still toiling on the climb and refuse to give up on themselves and their beautiful talents and abilities. I dedicate this book as a voice for those who have none, who boil inside with passionate, emotional energy, yet who never felt safe enough to express their true feelings. This book is their testament.

This book is also dedicated to my beautiful children: Peter, Allyson, Indianna, Benjamin, and stepchildren: Christopher, Micheal, and Caitlin. May this book help illuminate your paths.

.

Contents

Acknowledgements

I would like to express my sincere thanks to all the participants in the two research studies that form the basis for this book. Without their kind willingness to share their lived experiences, this book could not exist.

Appreciation and acknowledgements also go to my wife, Lisa, for her steadfast belief in me. Great things rarely happen in a vacuum and this book is no exception. Numerous people have expressed their support and faith in the need for this book and in my ability to bring it into being. I acknowledge and thank all for the warm support for myself and for the work ahead.

My thanks to Dr. Elaine Aron for providing a strong foundation of rigorous research that allows researchers like myself to extend discussions of sensory processing sensitivity to very practical areas like career.

.

Foreword

It is with such great pleasure that I introduce you to *Thrive: The Highly Sensitive Person and Career.* Whether you are searching for the right job or career, or already in one, we all work at something and as highly sensitive people, we all need to think about our work in terms of our trait. Above all, we need meaningful work. That means, ideally, work that suits you, as a unique and highly sensitive person.

A sociologist friend has likened Western (and increasingly global) attitudes towards finding the right career to attitudes about finding the right life partner—fall in love with the right one and you can be happy ever after. Until the last century, the choice of both spouse and job was made for largely practical reasons. Parents decided, or your location, social class, or economic situation provided you with few options. Today you choose with many more options, based largely on personal choice and emotions, than a hundred years ago. It is a romantic view, but in line with human progress towards each person expressing his or her traits, personality, talents, preferences, and maximally, self-actualization.

People have asked me why I did not write a book on high sensitivity and work, but I was too aware that many highly sensitive have "married" the wrong job and cannot handle the pain or cost of a "divorce." You have families or landlords counting on your income; you feel lucky to have any job at all; or you are just plain scared of making another mistake. I did not want to write a book in which I said, "Just go for it – HSPs must have meaningful work." We cannot always, especially given that we also need a workplace that is not too negative socially or overstimulating.

Tracy Cooper has taken on the huge task of explaining with great care how you might find the right work situation without so much pain. He has delved into it deeply, beginning by making this the topic of his doctoral dissertation. He took the qualitative approach, interviewing a number of highly sensitive people, and then asking a larger number of them whether they also found true the things he had discovered from his interviews. This is much like the approach I took when I began my research on highly sensitive people. I was always glad that I had interviewed at least 40 of them for several hours before I ever began any quantitative research. I still remember many of them.

The breadth of Tracy's coverage of careers is one of the best features of this book. He himself has that breadth of experience, from his beginnings in the U.S. Army in an air defense missile combat unit to working in school yearbook and printing companies to teaching college, earning his doctoral dissertation and becoming an author and consultant. Tracy knows what the meaning of frustrated potential truly is. But this is not about his past, but the future of the workplace and careers in general and how you can fit into that.

I particularly like this book's discussion of how HSPs might find meaningful work in one of the trades, which can be both satisfying and lucrative without so much formal higher education. This opens a door that an author with an entirely academic background would have overlooked. In effect, he is saying, "Have you considered these charmers over here as ones to spend your life with." Or if this is already your "partner," you can work on this relationship so that maybe you do not need a divorce after all. He also goes deeply into the values and problems of being self-employed or working at home for your employer. "These are real sweeties, but thoroughly know what you are doing before you propose."

Whatever your job or career, Tracy also walks you through the issues of self-care, always a problem for us, but especially at work because of overstimulation and being so open to the effects of the emotions of others. He ends with a number of stories of other HSPs, in their own words. This is almost like meeting other HSPs in person as the conversation turns to work. It truly helps you to feel you are in good company.

A particularly valuable emphasis in this book is the impact of childhood on how this trait affects your navigation of the world of work. This reflects the latest research on differential susceptibility – that sensitive people with a difficult childhood or stressful history will have greater difficulty (than those without the trait) with their emotional reactions to problems and simply being out in the world. Those with supportive childhoods, on the other hand, could be especially successful once they find their niche. Those without that support will have to work on themselves first to arrive at a similar place, much as Tracy has.

Tracy discusses his childhood difficulties, which occurred mainly at school, though at home as well. The subject of the impact of the school environment on children is often forgotten by researchers, but it affects HSPs tremendously, especially boys. Teachers often misunderstand sensitive children as simply being shy and therefore needing to be pushed, which usually makes things worse. Or they seem lazy because they lose interest in school, given the slow pace and lack of depth. Or they withdraw because of the overstimulation. Sensitive girls may do better in school by trying to please the teacher, but often have social difficulties which can replay in the workplace, along with a possible problem with speaking up with their creative ideas rather than conforming.

One implication is that if you are one of those who had a difficult start in life, through no fault of your own, you should not compare yourself to those who enjoyed an enriched family life or welcoming school environment. Another, happier implication is that sensitive people with more difficult backgrounds seem to heal from these wounds more quickly than those without the trait. Therefore, DO NOT despair. It may take you longer to reach where you want to be, but it is highly likely that you can do it. Tracy with his painful school experience finally found his way in midlife. My childhood problems were more at home, but as with him, it was not until midlife that I began researching high sensitivity, earned my doctorate, and gained my license in clinical psychology. Tracy and I both received some help and I think it fair to say that we are both doing well, at home as well as at work. Truly, do not give up. You have so much to offer, and let Tracy help you.

Lastly, *Thrive* is practical, including its emphasis on feelings, even if your work mostly involves your intellect. This is because the depth of processing that makes us search for meaningful work and produce such *good* work is motivated by our emotions, such as empathy, curiosity, and a desire to do things *right*. This emphasis on feelings will, I think, help your sensitivity feel right at home as you open these pages.

—Elaine Aron

Preface

"No man needs sympathy because he must work, because he has a burden to carry. Far and away the best prize that life offers is the chance to work hard at work worth doing."
~Theodore Roosevelt

Beginnings

"Work worth doing," that seems to be the great challenge so many of us face today as work is constantly redefined by technology, demands are made for greater efficiencies with less labor, and societies consistently fail to adapt to changing paradigms. This is especially true for highly sensitive people (HSP), who face unique challenges in matching temperament to career.

My story involves a series of ill-matched jobs over several decades, finally leading to a decision point at midlife where I knew I had to reconcile issues that had plagued me for all of my adult life, if I were to experience any sense of satisfaction in my working life. The ensuing journey involved my return to college, completion of a bachelor's degree, followed by a master's, and finally a Ph.D. What I was able to learn along the way illuminated a path that had been murky, confusing, frustrating, and unclear.

I have always loved to work, but encountered continual frustrations with incompetent managers, arrogant supervisors, and sometimes miserable co-workers. Many of the positions I held were extremely boring to the point of being emotionally and physically depressing, unchallenging in the sense of not engaging even a tiny fraction of my capabilities, and left me feeling like I had consistently worked well beneath my potential. Through it all, I felt a deep sense of frustration at being "different," at needing more creative challenges, autonomy, growth opportunities, and a working environment with a measure of personal respect than did those around me. My life as a highly sensitive person, and as a highly sensitive male, seemingly predestined me for a highly individual life, yet no guidance was available. Awareness of HSPs did not exist in the small American Midwestern town where I grew up and still does not.

I wrote this book to be an adaptation and extension of a study I carried out for my doctoral dissertation. Dissertations are notoriously difficult to read because they are aimed at a specific academic audience (the student's committee) and are intended to satisfy certain criteria in terms of organization and form. In short, they can be very boring to read! I determined to write a book specifically for HSPs that presented my findings in a more palatable way, plus add in the results of a second study I carried out post-dissertation in 2014, in the form of a survey that asked people questions based on the themes from my study. I include those results throughout the book along with my interpretations and additional analysis not possible in a dissertation.

This book is for *all* HSPs, regardless of education, background or future career intent. The picture we will weave together is of necessity complex, dynamic, and inclusive of a wide range of experiences. Whether your work requires post-secondary education or vocational training, our needs as HSPs are the same and all may benefit from the discussions ahead because the demands of life to have a career that works confronts and weighs on us all. I have worked in varied positions from being a member of the U.S. Army to throwing newspapers out of the window of a VW Rabbit. I have worked in positions that required simple repetition to others requiring high-level executive and organizational ability, while pushing me into areas I never thought myself capable of. Throughout the past three decades of life, none of my positions have lasted longer than four years. The resultant effects on my self-esteem, confidence, and explanatory style have been an ongoing struggle. I always had the sneaking feeling that "something was wrong with me." The journey to discover that, indeed, *nothing* was wrong is the genesis of this book.

Sensory Processing Sensitivity Explained

Sensory processing sensitivity is a personality trait first identified in the mid-1990s by researchers Arthur Aron and Elaine Aron[1]. The establishment of this distinct trait, different from introversion and shyness, was a lightning bolt of realization for many highly sensitive persons, who may have previously thought we were neurotic, shy, or introverted. Many of us lived partial truths, believing we had found "the answer" in introversion, but the establishment and subsequent rigorous testing of sensory processing sensitivity – including fMRI testing – provided the rest of the picture. Finally we had something that explained why we prefer to observe and think before acting; why we feel and process everything very deeply; why we may become overstimulated before others; why we are highly empathetic; and why we seem to notice subtleties before others.

Being a highly sensitive person is more than simply a tendency toward overstimulation. It is fundamentally being easily activated emotionally that leads us to feel and think very deeply. It is feeling the energy of other people, being able to take their position and experience their energy, even when we do not wish to. Being a HSP is being creative, not in the mundane sense of producing an end product, though many are in creative fields, rather *creating a universe of meaning, personally defined.*[2] With our natural propensity toward noticing subtleties, we are ideally built to live creatively, to think and do things others would never imagine. Highly sensitive persons may be gifted individuals, though not all are. HSPs may be introverted, extraverted, or both. To be an HSP is to be psychologically and emotionally androgynous, embodying complexity and a broad spectrum of what it means to be human. Being an HSP is to be fully awake in the present moment as a full-spectrum human being, capable of accessing and expressing a complete range of emotions and potentialities.

The Historical Context

Sensory processing sensitivity is not new, though the term itself is still relatively new. One fifth of the total population has always been highly sensitive. If we think for a moment of sensory processing sensitivity as one element in an overall survival strategy for the species, with one-fifth of the population more sensitive and aware than others, and we add in the historical viewpoint that we lived as hunter-gatherer tribes for most of our recent history, it is possible to see HSPs as members of a tribe where our unique sensitivities come into play to creatively solve everyday problems.

Imagine life in a tribe for a moment, you would live as part of a group of less than 150 members. Some would be hunters, while others would engage in gathering of foodstuffs from the local or extended area. Now imagine you are an HSP in this tribe and you are a gatherer. What advantage might your sensitivities hold? Your ability to notice subtleties before others might provide you with privileged knowledge because you noticed not only where certain plants grew, but also when they seemed to ripen. Further, because you think deeply and have a strong capacity for reflection, you have already planned for the right time to harvest this crop. In your daily wanderings you are more aware of your surroundings. You notice things others overlook, like shortcuts to move from one place to another or the location of a potable water source. You think of new ways to accomplish tasks and spend time, intuitively "knowing" how to prioritize and plan: you are likely a prized member of your tribe.

Now imagine you are on the opposite side of the fence as a hunter. What advantages might high sensitivity hold for you as a hunter? For one, you are probably good at reading animal tracks and signs, since you notice subtleties. You have run through various scenarios for how to track and kill the prey animals, which you may feel great compassion for and connection to. You may have even developed better tools or procedures to make the hunt more effective. During the hunt itself, your strong intuition and quick reactivity makes you a valuable hunter.

Or perhaps your role in the tribe is behind the scenes as the healer or shaman. In that role, your ability to enter altered states of consciousness more easily than others makes you valuable and useful to the tribe, because you are accessing ways of thinking and knowing others do not. Your role in the tribe is not limited by vocation. You are capable and proficient in your chosen or ascribed role because you are deeply conscientious. I use the analogy of the hunter-gatherer to illustrate the way HSPs likely fit into society as it existed long ago and to demonstrate the utility in being an HSP. Being alive has always entailed survival considerations and the personality trait, sensory processing sensitivity, is *directly geared toward that goal.* Moreover, it is geared toward overall survival of the species.

Our modern society is one of specialization, with individuals possessing less broad-based skills and with more intense, extended, and artificial social interactions. In a modern society, one is expected to be extremely social, enthusiastic, and optimistic, be a team player at all times, and question little. Conformity, emotional stability, and obedience are what is valued in a society based on the profit motive. Modern society has long been immersed in a *crisis of meaning*.[3] People experience more depression and anxiety now than ever before. Work is less stable, making frequent changes of employment almost the norm. How are HSPs to navigate this increasingly complex, less meaningful world of work and are there new opportunities on the horizon?

The Present Work

In this book, I present the results of two research studies conducted in 2014. In the first study, I interviewed thirty-five HSPs to better understand their experiences with careers.[4] In the second study, I asked questions in survey format, with possible responses provided in the format of strongly agree, agree, neither agree nor disagree, disagree, and strongly disagree, derived from the results of the first study to 1,551 participants. Using the results of both studies, I present distinct themes and provide detailed discussions of each one, including statistics denoting prevalence among the HSP population. It is worth acknowledging, at this point, that, neither the initial qualitative study nor the survey polled non-HSPs. I feel confident, however, by virtue of repetition of thematic mentions by HSPs, coupled with my experiences personally, and, as an HSP living among non-HSPs, that the findings are valid and provide an unparalleled depth of insight into the lived experiences of HSPs as they relate to career.

My intent, is for this book to be a very practical guide, based on solid academic research, which HSPs and non-HSPs can utilize to better understand this personality trait, or someone they know, as it applies to work and career. There are a number of well-meaning authors writing about what it means to be an HSP and how it may apply to career, but few are based in carefully conducted, peer-reviewed or vetted research that can be thought of as scientifically valid. I wrote this book to help fill that gap. It is my belief that few things can go well for us if we cannot get the issue of career right, because of the sheer amount of time per day most of us devote to work and the crucial importance of being able to provide for ourselves and families. I refrain from over-romanticizing the issue of work, because of the practical reality and diversity of our individual situations. I will, instead, offer pragmatic advice geared toward improvement in perception, circumstance, or tolerance, while offering cautious suggestions for potential "good fits."

I acknowledge the extreme difficulties many HSPs have encountered in the workplace, as they attempted to fit in to company cultures and workplaces that are often less concerned with providing the conditions that promote job satisfaction and more focused on the profit motive at all costs. Some have been beat down by oppressive workplaces and given up the struggle to find meaningful work. For those HSPs, I hope you find expression and healing in many of the quotes contained in this book and possibly find new energy to reshape your lives.

Throughout each chapter, I include representative quotes from study participants that illustrate each theme. Some are quite poignant and heartfelt, while others are starkly honest and demonstrative of the many challenges HSPs encounter in life. I invite the reader to enter the space created in this book and reflect on each theme. I have touched on many themes and some deserve entire books. Of the many themes, I consider the first three: empathy, childhood's influence, and self-care to be of prime importance, while the others seem to provide deep context within which we all live. It is my sincere hope that you find this book to be useful in discovering your own path. The painter, Chuck Close, offers us a piece of advice that I lived by while creating this book.

> *"The advice I like to give young artists, or really anybody who'll listen to me, is not to wait around for inspiration. Inspiration is for amateurs; the rest of us just show up and get to work. If you wait around for the clouds to part and a bolt of lightning to strike you in the brain, you are not going to make an awful lot of work. All the best ideas come out of the process; they come out of the work itself. Things occur to you. If you are sitting around trying to dream up a great art idea, you can sit there a long time before anything happens. But if you just get to work, something will occur to you and something else will occur to you and something else that you reject will push you in another direction. Inspiration is unnecessary and somehow deceptive. You feel like you need this great idea before you can get down to work, and I find that's almost never the case."* ~Chuck Close

With the impetus to derive our inspiration as we work, I invite the reader to read, reflect, and absorb the learning that is possible from this book, but, then, to move to a fuller expression of embodiment of their innate humanness beyond any HSP label. Whether you are an artist, engineer, scientist, software developer, teacher, nurse, carpenter, self-employed, unemployed, retired, or lost somewhere in between, seek out and become the fullest exemplification of who you are and know that, much as a spring flower in bloom, our time is limited to this single season of life. Inasmuch as life is truly about survival in a complex, complicated society, our inner drive to fuller and broader realizations of our potential implore us to move beyond survival to thriving!

How to use this book

This book is divided into three parts. Part one lays a foundation, detailing the ways work has changed and introduces important concepts referred to later. Part two deeply explores the ways in which HSPs experience work to better understand our needs. Lastly, part three offers advice on careers for HSPs and insights from HSPs. The book is best read from beginning to end, as it builds on the framework in part one. You may find yourself skipping between sections if you read books like I do. Each chapter contains a wealth of information I hope you find to be truly informative and useful in your life.

About me

I am not a psychologist, though I have delved very deeply into that area. Rather, I am a transdisciplinary scholar and researcher, which means I move beyond disciplines like psychology, sociology, creativity studies, and others to harness their knowledge, without being subject to their inherent limitations, while focusing on a real-world issue. My goal as a broad-based researcher is to extend the findings on sensory processing sensitivity (the underlying trait all HSPs have) into practical areas like work, career, and potentialities. I am less interested in description of the trait than in how it applies to our lives. It has already been described a great deal and solidified through fMRI studies and several peer-reviewed journal articles. With that basis, it is up to broader-based researchers and thinkers to extend the meaning of sensory processing sensitivity beyond pathology, into areas of life where the "rubber meets the road," so to speak, with no area being of more importance than HSPs and work.

In this book, you can expect less of the academic speak and more of the practical combined with the theoretical, as I bring you results of my studies, combined with everything I have learned and absorbed as a highly sensitive researcher and consultant to numerous HSPs and HSS/HSPs.

<u>Part I</u>

Setting the stage

Prior to embarking on this journey of HSPs and career, we need to, first, understand how work has changed in recent decades, so we can begin to widen our view of the possibilities that may exist for HSPs. With that in mind, part one of this book is all about the working world and begins with what I consider to be the unifying element that all HSPs can relate to: the experience of *flow*. More about this in chapter one, but regardless of our socioeconomic status or career choice, we can all experience the type of engagement of our extensive capacities, if certain conditions are in place.

Part one then moves into an introductory discussion of the interpersonal and physical working environments that HSPs related to me in two 2014 studies. You will note that chapter one includes the first of many survey results in block form. I placed each of these results strategically to relate to relevant sections. As you will see, many times the percentages were overwhelmingly strong for or against a question. These survey results are from a first of its kind quantitative survey and are presented throughout this book with much appreciation to all the 1,551 survey takers.

Author's note: you may notice I alternately use expressions like "an HSP," even though I defined it at the beginning as denoting "highly sensitive person." In this format I am bowing to the societally ingrained use of the term for ease of reading.

Chapter 1

Work

"We all desire to be what we are but are all too often prevented from acting out our being." ~Dante

"Acting out our being," highly sensitive people seem to desire this experience more than most, yet our experience of work is often fraught with complexities above and beyond what others encounter, making our working lives heavy with a number of obstacles that demand our careful attention and planning. HSPs are individuals with deep emotional lives, often exquisitely sensitive, strongly empathetic, innately creativity, and compassionate toward others. Whether we are aware we are HSPs or not, we work at all levels of society from the highest levels of leadership to technical professions, creative, education, healthcare, and trade work. Many are self-employed or would like to be. Some have found themselves so beaten by the vicious nature of some workplaces as to withdraw completely and seek solace in individual work far from the public eye. Other HSPs thrive in their work and can fully act out their being. In this chapter, we will, first, establish how the workplace has changed. Once we better understand this phenomenology, we will begin to explore some of the HSP-relevant points more deeply.

The Changing Workplace

It is not a secret that the workplace is changing in dramatic and far-reaching ways that impact all of us and future generations. The nature of organizations and companies has undergone radical transformations in the past few decades brought on by automation, increased competition from global sources, and changing cultural attitudes. Some of these changes are potentially in favor of HSPs, while others may be problematic. Let us look at a few ways companies and organizations have changed, then examine ways these may work for or against HSPs.

• Companies today are leaner and continually reorganizing as they seek to remain competitive or gain an advantage in the marketplace.

• Organizations today typically are not able to provide long-term security or stable employment, due to their focus on competitiveness and profit.

• Less of an emphasis on centralized decision-making structures and more on diffused authority. Managers may be more coaching oriented than authoritarian.

• More focused on value from the customer perspective.

As a result of these foci, the nature of work has changed in significant ways. Work today is:

• More cognitively demanding with greater inherent complexity.

• Focused on teamwork and collaborative strategies than individual efforts.

• More socially intensive, as collaboration represents the expectation.

• Demands technological competence, continually reinforced as technology continues to evolve.

• More time-sensitive, as companies focus on just in time systems and other efficiencies.

The Pro

These new built-in complexities in the workplace require skill sets HSPs may possess in abundance due to their innate temperament. For instance, the emphasis on cognitive and technological competence, synchronizes well with HSPs sense of curiosity and need for growth. Likewise, the team-based environment, may work well with HSPs strong empathy and inherent need to ensure tasks are well planned and executed. HSPs are deeply conscientious and have a strong need for things done well. HSPs are naturally creative, with divergent thinking virtually ingrained in their DNA. As companies seek innovation, HSPs should be well-positioned for problem-solving in new and novel ways. Lastly, HSPs seem to prefer working environments that are personally meaningful and facilitate professional growth. Ironically, the lack of inherent stability in many companies may mean one is no longer tied to the notion of lifelong employment where stagnation has already set in.

The Con

There is, of course, a downside to being highly sensitive in a modern workplace. Serving as a team member implies that one will have an equal part in all interactions and decisions. For some HSPs, simply speaking up and making their voices heard may prove difficult as they have learned from the past that others do not appreciate their original insights. HSPs may also suffer from low self-esteem, which would make working as a full team member reliant on the thoughtful composition of teams where an equal voice is given to each member and a safe environment of trust is firmly established at the beginning, is considered.

The emphasis on teamwork may also prove to be too socially demanding for more introverted HSPs, who prefer to work on their own with minimal supervision. This may be variable, though, with some compromise between solitary work balanced with more intensive social interactions. The lack of long-term stability in many companies may be anxiety producing and preclude some HSPs from feeling as if their working environment is supportive and capable of facilitating their overall professional and personal growth. Time pressures may also prove to be counterproductive as team members "look over the shoulder" of a highly sensitive person, which is strongly distracting. Deadlines, however, may be of value as HSPs structure and organize their time to meet expectations in a dramatically transforming workplace. One additional way workplaces are changing involves the notion of employees being on premises full-time, ready, and able to work on projects, leaving only at the end of a scheduled shift. Employers are constantly searching for new efficiencies, and one way they are finding to be very cost-effective is through the implementation of an on-demand workforce.

The new on-demand workplace

Most of us are familiar with the inventory systems at big box retailers, where merchandise is ordered as it rings up at the register and the customer takes an item home. The order is sent to distribution centers, which are strategically placed within a region servicing a number of stores. The item arrives within a day, or a few days, hence the "just in time" moniker. Now, that same idea is taking root with employers: instead of maintaining a large, static workforce of people in the office, an employee is called in to work only if needed. Often the employee is hourly, contract, or contingent, meaning that companies, for the most part, have no actual ties to them.

Employment in the 21st Century, means we may be associated with an external firm that contracts out their specialized labor pool to companies who can utilize such talent. Often companies do not have a long-term need for highly specialized labor, beyond a specific project, but many hourly workers begin as unskilled labor and are used to fill in seasonal labor gaps, then released once the work is caught up. Some workers work from home, thereby negating the issue of commuting to an office, but others are subject to the anxiety of not knowing if they will work on a given day.

More than a third of the U.S. workforce are now contingent workers, and the trend is expected to rise to half in the coming years.1 Clearly, there are some potential instability issues that would affect any worker, but HSPs, particularly those with fewer skills, may be especially vulnerable to anxiety, stress, and burnout due to fluctuations in income security. There is a potential upside as well, especially for highly skilled workers who are compensated well and allowed the opportunity to work from home, and to work on various projects. In fact, the short-term project schedule may work extremely well for one type of HSP: the high sensation seeker, which we will explore more in chapter six. One of the biggest benefits HSPs may experience from some contract, or contingent work is an increase in autonomy and freedom. HSPs strongly prefer autonomous work that allows them to enter an experience where their capacities are fully engaged, or a state called flow.

The experience of flow~

Flow is a concept developed by psychologist Mihaly Csikszentmihalyi, to encapsulate the experience we have when we are engaged in a task or project that causes us to stretch our abilities, to be fully engaged and aware in the moment as we pursue a challenging goal. The experience of flow can take place while performing any task, whether it is work, performing, parenting, sports, or any other activity that fits the criteria of causing us to become fully absorbed in the moment in pursuit of that worthwhile goal. When we are in such states, we lose all sense of self-consciousness, lose track of time, and push ourselves to grow. This capacity was likely evolved as a survival mechanism long ago, when those individuals who learned to push themselves toward challenging goals achieved a survival advantage over those who did not. In short, flow and the desire to be in a state of full engagement of our capacities is inherent in our species. For HSPs, the need to be in a state of flow seems to be even more imperative due to a temperament that is innately creative, curious, exploratory, deeply conscientious, and complex.

Csikszentmihalyi delineated eight characteristic dimensions of the flow experience:2

• Clear goals: an objective is clearly defined with immediate feedback on one's performance.2

• Personal skills are matched to the challenge.2

• Action and awareness merge. Complete focus of the mind

on the task.2

• Concentration on the task at hand; irrelevant concerns and worries disappear for the moment.2

• There is a sense of potential control; this is not actual control or mastery but perceived ability to fulfill the requirements of the task.2

• Entrance into a liminal space where growth can occur, ego is transcended, and self is subordinated to the experience.2

• All sense of time seems to disappear; hours may pass and be perceived as much less.2

• The experience becomes worth doing for its own sake or autotelic.2

Many of us only experience a sense of flow once in a great while but lose the expectation that our paid work can and should be about more than providing compensation for labor, even skilled labor. Our society seems to be obsessed with time and efficiency and instills limits early in life for how and when we engage our capacities. As a result, we lessen our expectations for flow experiences. Soon enough, work becomes drudgery and life loses its sparkle.

Flow for HSPs

For HSPs, the issue of flow is important because we are uniquely complex individuals with a natural predilection for challenging work that supplies growth opportunities and engagement. Too many of us grew up not being accepted for our sensitivity, not feeling like we are a part of anything, and not being presented with challenges that were worthwhile and matched to our abilities. Many of us are gifted, and feel like we are consistently under matched in terms of our abilities to a task, yet the need for successfully completed tasks that engage our full capacities, while imparting a sense of control (even if only perceived), is essential to our psychological health and well-being.

Many HSPs list boredom, and the threat of boredom, as high on their list of work-related concerns. Boredom is something everyone faces, to an extent, in their work, but for HSPs the boredom is processed more deeply, and many times felt somatically. Anxiety and frustration may also accompany feelings of boredom and lead to an inability to remain in a position for long periods of time. It is not uncommon for HSPs to be perennial job hoppers, leaving positions every few years, as they seek new stimulation and flow experiences. The accompanying sense of perceived emotional instability may be quite strong for some HSPs, as they pose the question to themselves "what's wrong with me, why can't I be like everyone else and just put up with the boredom?" The simple answer is, HSPs are complex, highly capable individuals who are not like everyone else in temperament and disposition. Our needs are simply different.

Flow applies to all HSPs

I chose to frame our initial discussion in terms of Csikszentmihalyi's conceptualization of flow because it is possible to experience flow in any job at any level. Flow is something that speaks to all HSPs, regardless of education, socioeconomic background, culture, or creed. An HSP working as a professional may be just as likely to experience flow as the HSP building a house, since the experience is keyed to the individual's abilities being matched to the task and imparting a sense of control. The good feelings that result from the experience of flow are more deeply processed in the HSP. Likewise, we may go to great lengths to avoid boredom, frustration, and anxiety through job hopping. We are forced to grow in complexity, because of our continuous need for flow-like experiences. The need to ever evolve is one of our major life issues, as we shall see.

The quotes you will read in this book are from HSPs working at every level of society. Some have found a balance in their work between flow and boredom, others have sought a better balance through self-employment, where there is more perceived control. There are several other important factors to account for in the way HSPs relate their working environments. Among these are the interpersonal and physical environments.

Interpersonal Considerations

Interpersonal relations are the big white elephant in the room no one wants to discuss. It's there, and it's touchy, moody, and potentially angry, so we just avoid it or minimize its impact, but there's no denying that the issue of interpersonal relations, and the co-occurring issue of emotional regulation, are among the top issues HSPs face on a daily basis.

Let us get right to the heart of why workplace interactions may be such a tricky issue for HSPs. Highly sensitive people have a personality trait that works through emotionality. An HSP experiences an interaction and let us say it's not a pleasant one for the sake of explanation, which then triggers an emotion. Those emotions may be positive or negative, even neutral, but in the case of negative emotions brought on by a less than positive social interaction at work, the person may experience anger, anxiety, frustration, or fear. Regardless of the emotion, what happens next is the stimulation gets processed very deeply in the brain, as the person plays the scene in their mind, over and over. It may be very difficult for the individual to calm herself when emotionally activated, and this may lead to somatic reactions, as the body begins to express what is being felt inside. In short, this person has been set off emotionally, often in a very short period and possibly unintentionally by the other person and is now in a very touchy emotional state.

In my survey 42% of HSPs agreed with the statement "managing my emotions is very difficult," 18% strongly agreed.

Some recent articles have exhibited the title "Do you cry easily? You may be a highly sensitive person." What they should have asked is "Do you go from zero to one hundred emotionally in two seconds? You may be a highly sensitive person!" The participants in my qualitative study mentioned experiencing anger, frustration, annoyance, irritability, and other anger-related terms on a much more frequent basis than sadness or being moved to tears.4 HSPs are not crybabies, we are emotional powerhouses! You are more likely to find us irritated than sad, angry than tearful, even passionately expressive than withdrawn and resigned.

Highly sensitive people experience a broader range and depth of emotions than others. Where others experience mere annoyance, an HSP may already progressed past annoyance and irritation to an intolerable state where relief must be found. This accounts in large part for HSPs need to recharge in quiet, and for quiet places to de-escalate from stimulation.

Don't get me wrong here, HSPs are not powder kegs waiting to explode at any given moment, in fact, we may be very good at hiding our emotional depth, but we do feel the energy of others more deeply and respond more quickly in an emotional sense than do others.

The significance of emotional reactivity in the lives of HSPs, is what led me to realize just how important the issue of self-care truly is, and why we need to develop ways of self-soothing that are tailored to our unique, individual needs, tastes, and environments. There are over a billion HSPs on the planet. What works for one hundred million, may not work so well for the next hundred million. Developing an awareness of our propensity for emotional reactivity is, however, paramount to all HSPs being more empowered.

Interpersonal Relations with Co-workers

The HSPs, in my study, expressed several important points about how they interact with co-workers that are important to unpack at this point in our discussion.

• HSPs have a strong dislike of superficial conversation and shallow individuals. This is likely due to an already full agenda of processing stimulation, with new stimulation being sometimes superfluous or irritating, to have to process as well. High empathy also means that HSPs prefer people of depth, with whom they can enter meaningful conversations. This does not mean HSPs are aloof or anti-social, rather, they may prefer to be more selective in joining conversations of no interest to them. HSPs, if engaged in a conversation of their choosing, may be terrific performers and be quite passionate or animated, and make extremely good communicators, because they are deep-thinking individuals, who are able to minimize chatty language. Customers, and others, may greatly appreciate this ability.

• HSPs strongly dislike arrogant or overly competitive individuals. People who are oriented toward constant competition, or smug arrogance, negatively stimulates HSPs, and they would rather avoid these types of individuals. That is not to say that HSPs are non-competitive, indeed, in the right context HSPs enjoy healthy competition, but they do not like to be surrounded by a savage mentality that places winning at all costs at the top of their lists of preferred working environments.

• Many HSPs prefer a one-on-one environment, where they can relate to and connect with one person at a time. Working on a one-on-one basis allows HSPs to utilize their deep empathy, connect with the other person in a deep way, and avoid excess stimulation which may come from interactions with groups or rushed situations. HSPs, however, may be very successful in any given situation depending on the individual.

In my survey, 40% of HSPs disagreed with the statement "I like to work in large groups or teams," 45% strongly disagreed.

• HSPs are deeply conscientious workers, who need for things to be done well. HSPs are likely your hardest workers and best planners who will be hard pressed to accept "good enough." This may lead to conflicts with co-workers for whom "good enough" is the acceptable standard.

• HSPs are innately creative and complexity-oriented. In the often-concrete corporate world, the focus may be more on achieving a given goal, without considering the long-term implications of poor design or poor planning. HSPs are hard-wired to view any problem from a multitude of perspectives and are clued into divergent thinking. This orientation may prove frustrating for HSPs, who find themselves in environments where real creativity is given token lip service, but not desired. Non-creative co-workers may also prove to be difficult to relate to.

• Highly sensitive people represent the breadth and depth of human expression and may be anywhere from mild to wild. Expecting HSPs to fit a preconceived mold or box is denying the reality that HSPs are all different from each other.

Interpersonal relations, for the highly sensitive person, are, at once, a source of strength and power, yet also a source of unwanted emotional energy and tension, that are ultimately as draining as empowering. You might say that we are emotional chameleons, taking on the color of the present moment, while simultaneously feeling the depth of its impact on the inside. It is true that HSPs are emotionally responsive individuals, yet we are also highly creative, deeply empathetic, and conscientious in ways others only dream of. Our interpersonal relationships with others may always be tricky, at best, but we also reserve a tremendous capacity for empathetic, open, and honest communications with co-workers and customers/clients that far outweigh any potential downside. The other half of this equation may equally support or detract from an HSP's working life: the physical environment.

The Physical Working Environment

There are many complexities to the actual physical surroundings we spend so much of our daily working lives in,

13

with much room for improvement or innovation. Many HSPs are quite familiar with their sensitivities to sensory stimuli, things like strong smells, uncomfortable lighting, distracting noises, and ergonomic issues, like cheap office furniture. HSPs are not alike; some may experience strong reactions to certain stimuli and not to others. There are, however, some common issues that HSPs expressed in my studies, such as a strong dislike of artificial lighting, lack of natural daylight, swings of temperature, from too hot to too cold, disorderly workspaces, sudden or unexpected noises, irritating noises, certain smells or odors, and the most strongly expressed: a deep dislike for open-office floor plan arrangements.

In my survey, 24% of HSPs agreed with the statement "I feel distracted or overstimulated by bright lights, strong smells, crowded office arrangements, or uncomfortable temperatures," 72% strongly agreed.

The various sensory sensitivities might be expected of HSPs, but the deep aversion to being forcibly crowded into an office arrangement, ostensibly to encourage and foster collaboration, ranks as the worst idea in modern times, and has been gaining ground among non-HSPs as well. HSPs, in the sense of being the proverbial "canary in the coal mine," whose job is to sense problems before they become issues for everyone else, seems to be fulfilled, in this instance. For HSPs, forced socialization detracts from their ability to concentrate, overloads them with unwanted sensory information, and imposes the energy of others onto their personal space, much the same as being on an airplane flight maddeningly crams people together, in a confined space, where civility hangs by a slender thread, at best.

14

Far from encouraging collaboration, open office floor plans have proven to be counterproductive and will likely fall by the wayside, as organizations continue to seek competitive advantage. If there is an upside to the way organizations function, it is their willingness to drop practices that do not increase or promote efficiency. The downside is this process is cyclical and may take time to filter down through organizational structures. Many times, HSPs describe managers who express indifference, hostility, or token acknowledgment of situations that do not work, but it is likely they are as caught up in bureaucracy and unable to make changes as the rest of us.

In my survey, 31% of HSPs agreed with the statement "I feel my employer just wants me to conform and do my work," 25% strongly agreed.

The built environment plays a huge role in setting the mood for the work that takes place in it. Issues like, the way spaces are arranged, the amount of natural daylight flowing through a space, how often the air is exchanged, and often overlooked issues like wall colors, amount and variety of plants, all contribute positively or negatively to the feel of a space, which is directly proportionate to how well people are able to perform. Of course, in some professions, there is less compromise possible on these issues, such as many of the healthcare, service, and retail professions, where the physical environment is built for functionality over other considerations. Examples include hospitals or a mechanic's garage.

In my survey, 26% of HSPs agreed with the statement "I prefer to have my own private space at work," 69% strongly agreed.

Some companies, however, are beginning to test

alternative office arrangements with features like, unassigned working spaces, quiet areas for workers to escape to when they need to, and meeting spaces big and small, for use by workgroups. These less structured arrangements, coupled with more diffusion of decision-making responsibilities and authority, represent a changing workscape, with plusses and minuses for HSPs, but what was expressed to me through both of the studies, conducted in 2014, with HSPs goes beyond a mere resolution of irritating issues to something larger. That something larger is meaningfulness in work.

Authentic Work

The one personality trait that has been demonstrated to exert any effect on job success is conscientiousness. What do I mean by conscientious? Conscientious individuals are disciplined, focused, organized, goal-oriented, deliberate in thought and action, reliable, and may be perfectionists when taken to extreme. Conscientiousness is a personality trait, but is related to achievement orientation, dependability, and orderliness.

In my survey, 25% of HSPs agreed with the statement "I am conscientious," 72% strongly agreed.

Below are representative quotes of HSPs citing conscientiousness:

What I've heard over and over..."you're very conscientious," and I think that's why they like me so much because, as a nurse, people die with people who aren't conscientious. (Hailey)

I am very quality-oriented, and if that means I step on people's toes, I step on people's toes and people don't appreciate

16

that...When you are an HSP and very conscientious and work focused it is very easy for coworkers to feel like we are unfriendly or aloof. I got that often. When they would tell you anything at all, it was that. Mostly they would not tell you and just acted. So, I was frequently very isolated (Evelyn)

I am always proud that I have never screwed over a customer intentionally...I never did anything with malice, and I gave great service. (Ava)

I want things done...I demand more, and people cannot understand...I can do much more than I expected myself, or what other people expect me to do. Very fast and very accurate. I like to have things done before the due date...so people respect me in a way, even never having a full-time job. They always ask me to stay. (Chouko)

On occasion, we are told to do something that we know is wrong, and we will bring it up, and they will say, "Oh, just do it anyway. It doesn't matter." Six months later it blows up, and they are like, "Oh my god, it's the end of the world!" and I am like, "Well, I told you six months ago that this was going to happen." We kind of know, or at least I do mostly because I have training. I look a little deeper and see what the repercussions are...When I am writing something, I like to keep it more simple, readable, and maintainable. (Seth)

Deeply conscientious people tend to be serious people who value recognition and respect for their efforts. They also tend to desire growth opportunities. Many HSPs report that they do not feel their efforts are recognized or respected and, further, that being afforded growth opportunities is extremely important to them. In fact, an impressive 88% of HSPs, in my survey, agreed or strongly agreed that learning new things is very important to them in their careers. Being able to do work that is meaningful, personally, professionally, and in a larger sense that serves others in egalitarian avenues, is important to most people, but seems to be especially precious to HSPs.

In my survey, 39% of HSPs agreed with the statement "I expect others to do their work to the same standards I set for myself," 45% strongly agreed.

Among highly sensitive people, the need to do work that is meaningful, that engages their creative capacities, that fosters a sense of competence and relatedness in one's field/s, denotes a deeper type of work that is, perhaps, best described as authentic work, or work that combines head and heart. The feeling of being somehow different than others in our society, further serves to set us apart, as a unique segment of the overall population. How does a quirky, creative, deeply conscientious, empathetic fifth of the population find temperament appropriate careers? Is self-employment the answer? My survey, indicated that 66% of HSPs would certainly like to work for themselves, if possible, but that's, perhaps, only a partial solution, because many people are not well suited to the rigor or demands of self-employment, nor do they possess the financial means to accept the risks entailed.

In my survey, 45% of HSPs agreed with the statement "I feel somehow different than others in my society," 48% strongly agreed.

In this introductory chapter, we have examined how organizations and companies have adapted their practices to become more competitive in a new marketplace that demands increased efficiencies to maintain competitiveness; and lean, adaptable workforces that are technically competent, socially adept, and capable of innovative, creative thinking and actions. We highly sensitive people are a unique group of individuals, who live in an intricate web of complexities. It is not possible for me to say, "All HSPs are like this," or "this solution will work for every HSP." Rather, it is necessary that we turn our attention to unraveling the web of complexity that is the lives of HSPs, through a close examination of the most important aspects of the life worlds we inhabit. Though this may seem reductive to some, the intent is to develop an in-depth understanding that other HSPs can use to create a better understanding of the contexts in which they live.

A proposal

I am a highly sensitive person and a sensation seeker. I have lived some 48 years on this planet and have devoted the second half of my life to the deep understanding of many of the issues we HSPs face, with the intent of developing practical knowledge that may help us better understand ourselves so that we may flourish. I propose to you that, if you read and reflect on the chapters in this book, it will help you with what I call the three A's: awareness, acceptance, and adaptation.

The first step to living our lives as HSPs, more fully, is to understand our true natures. Becoming aware of what it means to be a highly sensitive person is crucial to further development. To accomplish this, we must set aside our societal conditioning and come to a deep understanding of what it means to each of us to be a highly sensitive person. This is not an easy first step and requires that you do a fair amount of reading and researching. Fortunately, there are several helpful books and videos online to assist you in gaining awareness. From there, you will move to the next step very organically.

Acceptance of who we are, requires that we reflect on how being a highly sensitive person has influenced our lives and the choices we have made therein. You will likely come to view some choices as negative and some as positive. Many will ask themselves "how has being an HSP been a positive at all?" For many, life has not been easy, and you have suffered greatly, like leaving jobs because they were intolerable or passing up promotions because they would have been too overstimulating or exhausting. Many of us have difficulty saying no and setting boundaries, which causes us many difficulties. Coming to a point where you can accept yourself as-is requires that you forgive yourself for the poor choices you may have made, which may not have been poor choices at all, but rather defensive, while accepting that your future choices will be more informed and based on your new knowledge of your temperament as an HSP. Finding acceptance, can be aided by seeking out other HSPs through social media, meetup groups, or other avenues that will allow you to see that there are other HSPs out there, and that you are not alone. This new acceptance will go a long way toward becoming our most authentic selves, as we cast off parts that we find not to be truly representative of who we are.

Lastly, adapting to life as an HSP, with a more clearly focused lens, can enable us to be more of who we are and less of who we are no, or who we do not wish to be. All adaptations are made to enable a smoother functioning of a process. View yourself as a process that is ongoing and in a state of flux and change. HSPs are not only a process but are part of a system of processes in a larger society. Modern society may be guilty of a certain tunnel vision with regards to a preferred temperament type most suited to the needs of the corporate world, but HSPs are present in all occupations and already contribute their vast creativity, conscientiousness, and vision, even if not acknowledged, understood or appreciated. The task for HSPs, is to adapt their lives to better suit their needs. HSPs, above all other people, must break the bonds of societal conditioning and become their own persons.

Advice for HSPs

Q: I feel as if I have always worked beneath my abilities. Can I change this?

A: Yes, you can change this, but it will require that you change some of the perceptions you may hold that may be holding you back. HSPs are highly conscientious individuals with a need for things to be done well. Aligning our inner perfectionist with the external realities of the working world can be key to arriving at a compromise that works better for you. More on this in chapter 8.

Q: I am such a quiet person at work and feel like I am often overlooked when it comes to contributing feedback on important projects. How can I make my boss see that I have great ideas?

A: About 70% of HSPs are introverted, which means most of us are likely quieter, more observant individuals than others. Helping your boss understand that your ideas are not only good but likely well thought out with long-term implications taken into consideration will require that you make an inroad in some way. You may not feel comfortable presenting your ideas in a noisy conference room full of people. Try another approach that feels more relaxed for you like a detailed email or printed presentation you can deliver in person to your supervisor. Once you establish that your ideas are workable and generative, you may find your boss to be much more receptive and appreciative of your deep-thinking approach. Another approach is to enlist the help of supportive coworkers who can help present the idea as a group, thus taking some of the pressure off yourself. However, at times, we must be bold and speak up individually, even if our inner HSP is screaming to retreat! You may find the experience to be empowering. In another sense, we have an ethical imperative, as HSPs, to ensure that our company or organization makes full use of our abilities and talents. When we break out of our comfort zone and speak up, we are fulfilling that imperative.

Q: I have had a long string of jobs that never amounted to anything. I am middle-aged and fearful that I may never find a career that I can be happy in.

A: This book will help you understand some of the complexities in the working lives of other HSPs. Better understanding our needs as HSPs can be a great first step toward finding the right work for us. My advice is to read each chapter carefully and spend some time reflecting on each section. Middle-age is also a time of great opportunity for many HSPs when, for many, the children are grown and the pressures of providing may be lessened. If you have never found a niche that works for you, there is everything to gain by attaining greater awareness regarding the nature of your difficulties as you move forward in life. This book will help!

Everyone has been made for some particular work, and the desire for that work has been put in every heart. ~Rumi

Part II

What kind of HSP are you anyway?

Highly sensitive people vary a great deal regarding exact disposition. It is simply not possible for any two of us to be alike. We may share some general commonalities, like intense emotional reactions, irritation at some sensory stimuli, or high empathy (to name a few), but, within that, there are many possibilities for variation, by degree. What stands as a major issue for one HSP, may be a non-issue for the next HSP. Additionally, some of us are more extraverted, introverted, or high sensation seekers, as well as highly sensitive. Rather than attempting to make sense of the milieu of swirling preferences and inclinations, it is far better and more intelligible for you, if I, very carefully, unpack each of the major components that were communicated to me, by actual HSPs, in two scientific studies that I conducted in 2014.

Each of the succeeding chapters, in part two, is thematic, with quotes from selected study participants included to provide us with an intimate glimpse into their lives. Part two, is organized thematically with the first three chapters (empathy, childhood's influence, and self-care), ranked at the top, regarding relative importance.

Empathy, or the ability of an individual to deeply enter the experience of another person to, in effect, stand in another person's shoes, stands out as the number one issue HSPs expressed to me as, simultaneously, a blessing and a curse.

Childhood's influence stood out, as defining for HSPs, as well with lingering positive and negative implications. There are numerous studies documenting the link between childhood trauma and later anxiety, depression, fear, loss of potential, and a whole host of other emotional issues that directly impact our ability to live our lives fully. Many people gloss over this issue, thinking that what happened in our childhoods, cannot possibly be linked to our adult lives, but the link is there and was apparent in all the HSPs that I interviewed.

Self-care, emerged in a surprising way. I knew intrinsically, how important tending my own needs has been in my life, but I was not prepared for the intensity that others would express this same need. In some cases, self-care was so far down on the list as to be non-existent. Those HSPs were, not surprisingly, burned out, alienated regarding their career, and, at times, very pessimistic about the future. The pain I felt from the descriptions of many HSPs bottoming out stories convinced me that, the only way many of us will be able to function well in our daily lives, is to elevate self-care to a spiritual practice. This may seem elementary, but too many of us suffer, because we do not take it seriously enough. I, at least, advise a thoughtful appraisal of your self-care practices, weighing whether what you are currently doing to remain calm, healthy, and balanced is sustainable in the long run. If it is not, changes in this area will help significantly with stress and overall balance.

The subsequent chapters, in part two, occupy equal footing, in my view, because of the web of complexity for HSPs, while extensive, is still one web, with each of us at the center. By carefully parsing out each point, I hope to provide you with a thoughtful construction of each concept and offer glimpses into the lives of HSPs. Any one chapter is informative and thought provoking and, no doubt, you will want to read each chapter, then spend some time reflecting on the impact of each in your life. This book is a book for HSPs, written by an HSP. I feel the impact of each theme in my life, just as you do.

Chapter 2

Empathy

"Empathy is about finding echoes of another person in yourself."
~Mohsin Hamid

Empathy defined

Many people do not realize that there is a difference between empathy and sympathy. Sympathy may be thought as the light version of empathy, where one acknowledges the difficulties of another person, without entering their experience. Empathy, by contrast, is directly entering that person's experience, and relating to them on a deep, human level of shared commonality.

For HSPs, empathy means picking up on and absorbing the emotional states of others, those that are expressed through facial expressions and body language, and those that are radiated out through emotional energy. The highly sensitive person is uniquely aware of subtle energies that others typically are not. At times, this may be overwhelming, as in the case of negative energy. Because HSPs process all experience more deeply than others, negative energy tends to affect us more deeply and for a longer period.

In my survey, 44% of HSPs strongly agreed with the statement "I have left positions in the past due to negative co-workers or superiors," while 26% agreed.

Empathy, in the context of the workplace, may be viewed from various angles, including the challenges and potentiality. Throughout this book, my emphasis will be, to express the personality trait, sensory processing sensitivity, from a strengths perspective, while acknowledging inherent obstacles. Empathy is, to some degree, present in all people, but it is especially strong in HSPs and may prove to be the most difficult issue to manage.

In my survey, 50% of HSPs strongly agreed with the statement "when I enter a room, I can immediately sense the energies of the people within," while 41% agreed.

The experience of empathy

What is it like to be high in empathy? For the highly empathetic person, life in the workplace may be a minefield of social interactions, with each new experience proving to be either energizing or draining. Consider the following quotes as representative of high empathy.

I was always very intuitive. When I walked into a room, I could gauge the emotion in the room. (Emily)

I notice things about people. I notice their eyes. I can; I know it sounds a little weird and crazy, but I notice aesthetics, and I notice things...this guy Gary...one day I was babysitting for Betty, and she told me Gary is not allowed to see the boy anymore. I found out that he was a pedophile, and I was like so sad. I knew something was wrong with him, but as a child, I did not say anything. All I could do was protect myself. I felt a lot of guilt that I could not have saved that little boy from being assaulted that I babysat for. (Taylor)

It is tough enough to be told that you are too sensitive, but I felt overwhelmed with all the kids and how intense they are. It was very negative energy for me. I was pretty much a loner from the very beginning in the sense of being around a bunch of people all the time, but when I was probably two years old, I could sense people who were kind. It drove my mom nuts because I would walk up to people in diners and stuff...and I would put my hands up like, "Hey, pick me up," it drove my mom mad. She was afraid I would do that to the wrong person, but I sensed at a very young age who was kind and who was not. (Makayla)

I am like a chameleon, whatever mood somebody around me is in I pick up on it. I'm trying to be a little better about it now that I'm aware of it, but I'm very easily influenced by other people's moods and where I'm working now most of us are out in an open pit, there's two, three, four of us in one big open area...so if one of my coworkers is in a bad mood, I will definitely pick up on it, and it definitely affects me. (Andrea)

I tend to internalize the states that other people are in around me. Sometimes I do not realize. I may not feel like I am being affected at the moment, but if I have a day or two away from it, I can kind of see that this has really been with me. (Kirk)

I was more motivated by knowing the customer and maybe being sensitive to their needs and not wanting to push too far. That seemed to be a struggle for me more than anybody else. Being sensitive to how or what people are like. We had customers who were like do not try to sell me any single thing, and I was very sensitive to that. We have to go out in the aisles and talk to people in the supermarket, and I was very sensitive about that. I did not like people doing that to me in the aisle. I did not want to do to people what I did not like done to me. (Morgan)

For Taylor, the experience of empathy served to warn her of the ill intentions of others. For Makayla, her ability to sense what others were like, extended to the positive and she was able to intuit a non-threatening person. Concurrent with the ability to sense what others are like, is the effect their energy or behavior may have on the highly sensitive person. Andrea describes herself as a "chameleon," and is deeply affected by the cognitive, affective, and emotional states of others. Her description of an open office must surely invite cringes from many HSPs, and bewilderment from those who dream up office plan schemes to encourage collaboration and creativity. Who would not want to participate in a constant, free flow of ideas and socialization, right? For HSPs, the constant absorption of energy from other people can be draining instead of inspiring, even for the thirty percent of HSPs who are extraverted. HSPs are energy chameleons and reflect the feeling of an individual or group, even of a space.

Intensity

All people, to some degree, experience empathy. As social creatures, we are built to cooperate and nurture others. We do this through anticipating and reacting to the emotional states of others, as expressed through their facial expressions, emotional energy, and body language. HSPs happen to be anatomically more attuned to the affective states of others and experience deeper intensity of the experience. It is the intensity with which HSPs are hit by the energy of others that can overwhelm. Highly sensitive people may struggle with understanding how to manage the overstimulation, how to avoid the experience altogether, and how to protect themselves from toxic situations.

Seventy percent of HSPs strongly agree with the statement "I seem to be more deeply affected than others by negative people at work," while 24% agree.

The intensity of a HSP's emotional reaction to empathy may prove startling to others, as if the person is overreacting, as compared to themselves. For the HSP, the intensity began with the triggering of emotion, that led to deep processing in the brain, quickly building to a possible crisis point, if the stimulation is particularly negative, or the individual is especially arrogant or offensive. Learning to manage the intensity of the moment may help, but the propensity for high reactivity will always be there for the HSP.

Seventy percent of HSPs strongly agree with the statement "I am sometimes overwhelmed by the energy of a room full of people," while 25% agree.

The gift of empathy

Empathy, as described above, may seem more like a curse than a gift, but being affected emotionally by others is only one aspect. Empathy may also be used to advantage in the workplace, where human interactions occur on a near non-stop basis. For example, those working in customer service capacities, the implications are vast for those who can understand and relate to the plight of the customer. As much as customers want their problem resolved, they also want to know that someone is really hearing them. In this regard, HSPs, if they can manage the initial intensity of their reaction to new situations, may be at a distinct advantage and may make excellent customer service employees and managers at all levels. You might think this to be counterintuitive, given that seventy percent of HSPs are introverted, but I invite you to think of HSPs as more than social or non-social. In fact, most people fall in between introverted and extraverted. HSPs may make very good "performers" and play the role of extravert quite well due to their creative and intuitive natures.

Here, Lily describes how empathy provides her with an advantage in her work:

My strengths are in communicating verbally. I can calm anybody down over the phone. I can keep a customer when they are losing a customer. I am very persuasive over the phone and very soothing to people. It is something that has served me well in those jobs.

Lily's high empathy allows her to connect with customers and ascertain how best to help them more easily.

31

Perhaps, more importantly, she can communicate to them that she is there, that she understands, and that she cares. Caring is a major asset, in any capacity, because it enables and nurtures bonds between people, enhancing customer and employee loyalty.

Respecting and connecting with others

Connecting with others, especially helping others, can be tremendously fulfilling for anyone, but, especially for HSPs. The sense of satisfaction and knowledge that one's work has an impact and matters in very tangible ways, likely sets up a positive feedback loop that HSPs benefit from. The moment of realization is demonstrated here by Julia.

I worked as a nurses aid in a nursing home once, and that was probably my most enlightening experience...where I felt compassion for the residents and felt like I really actually could make a difference in their lives, as I looked around at the younger and less mature nurses' aides and how they treated the patients and what I could see in the patient and what they couldn't see. You know, that, hey, there really is a person in there, and they have dignity. (Julia)

Learning to connect with others through empathy can be confusing, at times, because one must learn to read everyone's facial expressions and body language. Dale's experience of working with performers, in a group setting, routinely required that he "read" each person. As he explained:

I am sensitive to other stuff in the environment too. Just the emotional energy, it really creates challenges for me in working in a theater because I am always around groups of people, and there is always a bunch of emotional energy going on. I will be conducting rehearsal and picking up on little subtle emotional changes in people in the rehearsal, and I have to try to filter that out, or I have to sort of say, ok this person may looking at something and frown and that can be a simple look of concentration not a frown of anger or frustration. (Dale)

Another example: Seth works in an office with other software programmers, and he often finds himself using his strong empathy to inform him when others "just aren't getting it," and change his approach, when he is attempting to address an issue or instruct. Being highly empathetic can be utilized in several instrumental ways. Hailey, for instance, is a nurse who cares for sick children and depends on empathy to alert her to a patient's needs.

If they are hurting, I can hear, if they are hot in their breathing, I can tell because I am so sensitive to them. I can see in their faces if they look like they are in distress. They can be happy too! I have monitors too, and I can tell any fluctuations because I am keen to noticing changes.

Empathic people can be individuals others seek out due to their ability to connect. As Hailey again relates:

They liked me, they liked to talk to me, and open up to me. I have a gift that people like to open up to me. If I can be calm and listen, they like to talk to me, and they still do. People confide in me.

The potential for connecting with others, helping them with their problems, or just being involved in a helping profession leads many HSPs to enter careers that help others. Education has long been known to provide some of the most satisfying work, with college professors and other teachers, routinely ranking high on the job satisfaction scales. HSPs tend to value meaningful work, deep connections with others, and a good deal of autonomy in carrying out their tasks. As a sometimes college professor, I can attest to the fulfillment of participating in not only the education of an individual but also the mentoring.

Empathy in the workplace: The challenge

There are many trying situations for highly empathetic people, in the workplace. Absorbing the negative energy of others, absorbing unwanted energy from interactions, and simply soaking up too much energy from other people, is very draining for many HSPs. How does one manage this defining aspect of being an HSP?

There are several key points that emerged from my research regarding empathy:

1. HSPs are more deeply affected by negative individuals, interactions, and environments that hold negativity.

2. HSPs may suffer greatly, on an emotional level, from negative interactions, which may lead to burnout and alienation. In those cases, HSPs may strongly desire to leave a position, or otherwise distance themselves, from the sources of negativity.

3. HSPs are, conversely, as affected by positive interactions and energy, as by negative energy. Thus, an HSP needs to seek out positive environments as much as possible and intentionally distance themselves from negative environments when possible.

4. Most HSPs, in my study and survey, indicated a strong liking for one-on-one interactions with others. This propensity can be quite valuable in the workplace, where one is able to function in this way.

5. The need to protect oneself from emotional pain was

felt and expressed very strongly, by the HSPs that I spoke with. I will cover more about this need in chapter three.

Advice for HSPs:

Q: I often pick up on the energy of others at work even when I do not want to. What can I do?

A: As highly empathetic individuals, we need to protect ourselves, as much as possible, from negative energies. In a work situation, of course, we do not have much of a choice and many times must absorb it. In that case, HSPs need to learn self-soothing skills and practice self-care religiously. When we know we will be absorbing unwanted energy, we need to be aware of how draining it is and plan to do activities that are calmer or find a period to rest in quiet.

Q: I often am aware of something being amiss at work before others know it. I am hesitant to say anything because I do not want to cause waves. How can I manage this feeling of being the canary in the coal mine?

A: It depends on the receptivity of those around you. They may appreciate your abilities or cast you as a troublemaker. If they appreciate your ability to notice difficulties before others it can be a great asset, but, if they are unappreciative, you may not be well-received and will have to use your judgement based on the risk of saying nothing. Again, it may prove useful to enlist others, so there is some solidarity as to the issue. In some cases, everything may work out, in others one would be wise to seek other employment, rather than stay in a toxic work environment.

Q: I feel so burned out from the negative energies at work and do not know how to make it any better.

A: HSPs often stay in jobs longer than we should, even when we know it is not healthy, due to financial need, fear of starting a new job search and all that entails, and loss of coworker friendships. When HSPs are truly burned out and need a change, we should not remain in situations that do not work for us. I do not advocate quitting a job, but, if possible, search for a new job while you are still employed or take on side projects, until they are viable enough to replace your current income. In some cases, self-employment is the way to go for HSPs. I will cover that much more in chapter 8.

Chapter 3

Childhood's Influence

"He carried his childhood like a hurt warm bird held to his middle-aged breast." ~Herbert Gold

The role of early environment

One of the biggest factors none of us have control over is our early childhood environment. Many people might say "what happened in childhood was so long ago, it can't possibly affect me now!" After all, we are grown-ups and make our own choices, right? The impact of our early environments is well known in the psychological community, with early trauma leading to a significant potential for anxiety, depression, low self-esteem, low self-efficacy, an external locus of control, poor overall physical health, and diminished realization of potential. The important thing to know is highly sensitive people are more deeply affected by negative environments. An early invalidating environment, or one that fails to meet a child's need for love, affection, nurturing, and parental response to one's needs, may become a lifelong battle with fear, pessimism, and internal strife.

Conversely, HSPs may experience a supportive childhood, where their needs were met, they were loved, cared for, and encouraged to try new things. Just as negativity is more deeply processed, positivity is also deeply felt and held onto. HSPs, from supportive backgrounds, tend to experience less fear at trying new things, because of the early validation leading to more optimism, a lower propensity for anxiety, depression, and a greater likelihood for healthy self-esteem, an internal locus of control, high self-efficacy, greater realization of overall potential, and overall better health.

37

So, what determines if I had an unsupportive childhood? One does not need to have had a completely chaotic, traumatic, or abusive background to be considered unsupportive. The criteria have more to do with the depth of impact these types of issues impart than in overall prevalence. The highly sensitive person is more deeply affected than others by early trauma and may hold onto that trauma, or at least the fear, isolation, and sense of disapproval. Determining if you had a supportive childhood is likely a bit easier because you instantly recall less negativity. Determining if you fall somewhere in between may be more difficult because many people experienced some degree of trauma, chaos, or abuse, but it was not necessarily extreme. For instance, I grew up during the 1970s, when it was common practice in the small-town Midwestern region of the U.S. that I grew up in to spank children regularly. Some of you middle-aged HSPs (like myself) likely recall being "switched," or spanked with a slender tree branch, even having to cut your own switch from a tree! Is that enough to think of your childhood as unsupportive? For some HSPs, this sort of trauma, depending on severity and frequency, may have contributed to anxiety and distrust of parents or other caregivers. Couple that with other issues and you might conclude that your childhood was a 50/50 mix, as is my case.

In my survey, 25% of HSPs strongly agreed with the statement "my childhood was not a supportive one," 25% agreed, 2% disagreed and 10% strongly disagreed.

Even if our early home life was supportive, most of us begin school and encounter a totally new and more socially intense environment that can result in trauma. I recall very vividly crying as soon as I reached the playground each morning during my first year of school. Many kids cry, but mine was as much at the overwhelming emotional energy given off by hundreds of kids on a noisy playground as a desire to return home where it was familiar and safe. Later, as my adult teeth began growing in, I developed an overbite with crooked front teeth. Being different in any way subjects many kids in school to ridicule and bullying. I was no exception, and suffered several incidents of ridicule by certain students early in my school career that colored, not only how I thought of myself, but also about school.

I wanted to be invisible, though I loved learning. I wanted to be away from students who did not accept me, but in public school, that is not an option. My self-esteem was damaged severely, and it took many decades to feel healed, to feel "whole." Early trauma can easily come from our school experiences, as well as at home. In fact, it may be easier to suffer such experiences in school because of the amount of time per day spent there, and the many opportunities for ridicule. Compounding the feeling of overwhelm at school, may be a sense of being somehow different, which may not have been so apparent at home. In time, children can develop a spider web of confusing thoughts about their self-worth and their identity. Is, indeed, something "wrong" with me, is the question many HSPs ask themselves.

What does an unsupportive childhood look like?

Now that we have established support or nonsupport in childhood as one of the most significant dividing lines separating HSPs, let us look a bit deeper. Hailey describes life with her mother:

"I didn't go to school very much. My mother was a very sick person, and that is who ended up in the 70s getting custody of us. It did not matter then; men did not get custody of their kids. So, as sick as she was I ended up with her and being the oldest I was expected to stay home and help care for these my younger siblings while she was, you know, involved in whatever people

like her do, usually its bad things." (Hailey)

In my survey, 25% of HSPs strongly agreed with the statement "the household I grew up in was often chaotic," 25% agreed, 24% disagreed and 10% strongly disagreed.

For a highly sensitive child, in Hailey's position, one can imagine how issues of anxiety, depression, hopelessness, learned helplessness, and pessimistic explanatory style can develop. The space that children receive from supportive parents, in which to grow into a healthy, balanced person simply did not exist for Hailey, who described lifelong issues with anxiety and trust of others.

I was always fractured. My adoptive parents had great issues. They were uneducated and simple people. What we might call unenlightened people having their own struggles and issues in life. My entrance in their life was more problematic than it was a blessing apparently. I was mostly neglected for the most part. They were not supportive and loving. Basically, I was just there invisible with little spurts of affection. (Julia)

Julia's expression of feeling "fractured" seems to capture what it means to experience an unsupportive childhood best. Lily described her parents as "actively neglectful" and any overreacting was instantly corrected. For the highly sensitive child, who is innately highly reactive, this stifling of a natural (for an HSP) instinct may be highly detrimental. Parents may confuse reactivity with weakness and overcorrect behaviors, as they act within socially constructed paradigms of "right" behavior. This may be especially true for the parents of highly sensitive males, especially fathers, who may fear their boy is gay. Though no one, to date, has provided reliable statistics regarding the percentage of gay HSPs, it is presumed to be generally about the same as in the non-HSP population.

In my survey, 31% of HSPs strongly disagreed with the statement "my parents were supportive of my sensitivity when I was growing up," 31% disagreed, 14% agreed, and 4% strongly agreed.

Non-acceptance of sensitivity, is there a double standard for boys?

Parents may not always understand sensitivity. They may be sensitive themselves, but have no knowledge of personality traits, beyond what they fear their child is abnormally displaying. The pressure to conform is a very powerful social force that drives many parents to approve of some behaviors and disapprove of others. At other times, a parent may be projecting their hidden feelings about their own sensitivity, which they may not even be aware of. In the sociology class, that I sometimes teach, I tell my students that the single biggest factor that separates how we experience life is gender. Concerning sensitive children, the relative acceptance of sensitivity, is largely divided similarly with girls being more accepted for their sensitivity and boys strongly rebuked. Overall, 74% of HSPs, in my survey, felt their sensitivity was not accepted when they were growing up.

In my survey, 37% of HSPs strongly disagreed with the statement "I feel like other people understood and accepted me as a sensitive persons when I was growing up," 37% disagreed, 9% agreed and 1% strongly agreed.

Why is it more acceptable, even expected, for girls to display emotion and not boys? The answer is gender. Gender is a socially constructed set of qualities assigned to a sex. Because they are socially constructed, they are arbitrary and specific to any given culture. Thus, one culture may value very aggressive, competitive, fairly emotionless males, while another may place less value on these qualities and instead emphasize cooperation, nurturing of others, and a more egalitarian

41

display of emotions between the sexes.

In the U.S., the culture is decidedly extraverted, aggressive, and competitive,, with emotions considered a weakness. For males, this denial of a significant portion of our human psyche is very detrimental. Male HSPs suffer more overall disapproval from parents, especially fathers, for displaying emotional sensitivity. Males may experience a double-dose of disapproval as they are roundly rejected for being sensitive and not "man enough," plus, possibly experience an otherwise unsupportive childhood. Sometimes, the criticism is overt and specific, other times it is general and vague, yet palpable:

I could never please my father. He was verbally and physically abusive to me, maybe because I was the first born, I do not know. I am not sure; it always felt like there were expectations. (Joshua)

I had the perception that everybody was like me, especially as a boy as I started working through the grades in school. It became more obvious through experience that sensitivity was something that I needed to keep to myself. It was basically a punishable offense, not in school, but with my dad. He was not respectful of that trait in me at all. I began to understand that it was unusual, and I began to understand that it was not acceptable both in terms of how I got along with the other boys and girls to a certain point. (Kirk)

Social pressures to conform are extreme, for parents and children. For the highly sensitive male, conforming to the expectations of others, often means suppressing an entire part of himself. Carl Jung, the Swiss psychiatrist and psychotherapist, developed the concept of the "shadow" to metaphorically contain the elements of ourselves that we suppress or otherwise hide away in our drive to fulfill societal demands. It was Jung's belief that these shadow elements may reemerge throughout our lives as our psyche seeks to reintegrate itself. In effect, males learn to deny the most human side of themselves. Female HSPs, on the other hand, may be more accepted by parents and others for exhibiting emotional sensitivity, though the participants in my survey clearly felt their sensitivity was not understood or accepted while they were growing up.

My parents were very supportive, does that give me an advantage over other HSPs?

In effect, yes, a supportive early environment does provide a greater sense of self-esteem, higher self-efficacy, less anxiety, less depression, and a higher sense of self-confidence when attempting new things. Early support and validation, provide a sense of resilience, that those from unsupportive backgrounds fail to develop:

I think, because my parents put their internal operations before anything else, they were always incredibly supportive of both my brother and I. (Olivia)

They have completely dedicated their lives to my brother and me, and they pretty much let me join any activity that I wanted to. I took archery and all different kinds of outdoor activities when I was a kid. They embraced me for being different. Mom and Dad when I got home, they liked being a safe haven. They were very loving, very supportive. (Makayla)

We had a very quiet, middle-class life. We did not have trauma. We did not have anything like a lot of the kids I saw. My parents were still together after 52 years. (Lucy)

I believe I am blessed with my father because he is a philosophy teacher, religion professor so he kind of exposed us to many different opinions and cultures and religions, which I believe is a blessing. (Aubree)

Makayla's parents embraced her for "being different" and supported her forays into various activities. Participation in activities, whether it be sports, arts-oriented, or otherwise enables and facilitates greater self-confidence and social ability. HSPs, from supportive backgrounds, start out with a firmer foundation on which to build the rest of their lives. This does not mean they still do not experience problems; just that they are more resilient – able to bounce back from obstacles while growing from the experience – than their unsupported counterparts.

The story does not end there...

As with many aspects of the highly sensitive person, plasticity plays a significant role in overcoming an early lack of support. The good news is that, even if you experienced an unsupportive childhood, you may largely overcome it! Partly, this may occur through simple maturity, as our shifting perspective reframes and refocuses early experiences. For others, therapy may be extremely useful in working through childhood issues and clearing the way for a fuller realization of potential. Certainly, when we begin work, we find that our accumulated emotional baggage is best left at the door, to focus on the job. For the most part, this tends to minimize the impact of the early environment. Many HSPs, from unsupportive childhoods, go on to very successful trades, professions, and careers. The propensity for anxiety, depression, and faulty perception is what lingers and surfaces from time to time.

Advice for HSPs

Q: My supervisor sometimes personalizes criticism, and I feel very hurt when that happens. How can I communicate

that personal criticism of any kind is extremely damaging to me?

A: First, no one should ever criticize another person's performance at work, by criticizing them as a person. To do so is unprofessional, mean-spirited, and manipulative. It is fair to critique an employee's performance. Indeed, critiques which look at technical, creative, and interpersonal aspects can be very helpful in enabling one's growth. On no occasion, though, should a supervisor resort to demeaning an employee. In some cases, the supervisor may be unaware of their tone and a simple reminder may be enough to change the behavior. HSPs especially benefit from positive feedback. An employer should always include positive comments in addition to pointing out areas for improvement.

Q: The company culture at my company feels like an extension of high school. I do not want to be stuck with the title of the "quiet guy," forever, but I see no way to make it change.

A: One study indicated a correlation between perceived quietness and reduced expectations. What that means is, if you're known as a "quiet" person your superiors may already have reduced their expectations for what you can accomplish (fair or not), this presents you with a huge opportunity to put your deep-thinking talents to work and develop a project or plan that may make a bigger impact than for someone whom it is expected from. Take advantage of that perceptual error and do not be afraid to wow them!

Q: My childhood was bad with trauma, conflict, and abuse. How do I heal from that while spending so much time at work?

A: Work indeed does become like a surrogate family group and, like any family, some members need room for healing and growth. Certainly, seek out employment at a company where the culture feels supportive and warm. HSPs will instantly pick up on a dysfunctional company culture. Work to put yourself in positions where growth is possible. Meaningful work that engages your intrinsic talents and abilities will help increase your self-esteem, self-confidence, and impart a feeling that you can control the course of your own life. Alternatively, work that is predictable and stable may provoke less anxiety, which may help you heal over time.

Chapter 4

Self-Care

"To experience peace does not mean that your life is always blissful. It means that you are capable of tapping into a blissful state of mind amidst the normal chaos of a hectic life." ~Jill Bolte Taylor

The need

After learning of the extent to which other HSPs are affected by empathy, overstimulation, and stress I quickly realized self-care had to be emphasized and included as a top-three theme. The experience of empathy and sensory sensitivity, combined with possible issues of early childhood non-support, is wearing, draining, and stressful for many highly sensitive people. Even HSPs, from supportive early environments, may be worn down by the demands of the pace society sets for us, as we strive to keep up with our daily needs.

HSPs, because we tire of social interaction, certain types of sensory stimulation, and the rush to get everything at work completed yesterday, need to approach self-care in a different way than others. I feel the issue of self-care has risen to the forefront more in recent years, but for many people, it still takes a backseat to the strictly instrumental aspects of daily life, where time is our master and our days are planned and regulated. The approach we need to take is this: self-care comes first. If we cannot keep ourselves in balance physically, emotionally, mentally, and spiritually we cannot hope to function from a center of well-being.

For many HSPs, this may seem like a luxury, but let's remember the reason Dr. Elaine Aron began investigating the trait – which eventually became sensory processing sensitivity – was because she noticed that half of her psychotherapy patients seemed to be "highly sensitive." They were seeking her out because they were unable to cope with life, unable to find or maintain a balanced center. In this chapter, I will lay out for you several of the key issues as they emerged from my study.

I must protect myself!

Protect oneself from what you might ask? A few examples below might help illuminate this strong need expressed by HSPs:

I learned very young to literally shut out everything around me and just go to a book. That was pretty much how I spent every moment, almost like I was being forced to interact with people because it was my only real escape, my only relief from it. I knew that everybody else did not feel like that so, of course, as a small child, I felt very like there was something wrong with me. I knew I was different, and I thought I was just a bad person, so I just crawled into myself for a very long time. I did not have a lot of friends. I did not really go places. I did not really do stuff. (Samantha)

In my survey, 49% of HSPs strongly agreed with the statement "I feel a need to protect myself emotionally from others," 42% agreed, 3% disagreed and less than 1% strongly disagreed.

I was interested in how deep introversion affects career choice, so I prompted Samantha to explain that a little more. She replied:

I have a very primal motivation that I do not want other people to have the childhood I had. I do not want people to have the life I have had. That underlies an enormous amount of what I do. I was treated in very unfortunate and unpleasant ways, and I will be damned if I will let that happen to anybody else. There is a huge protective streak. There is a huge sense of wanting to make life better, and there is a huge sense that each of us has something of importance. I spent a lot of time being told that I was over-sensitive, and that I was immature, and that I was this, and I was that. To look back on all of that and say all of these things have created a person who generally speaking is pretty damn empathic and is able to walk in other people's shoes and help other people out and let other people see another perspective that is playing to the world that I have created. My whole motivation is that I do not want other people to live the life I have had to. I want them to have a better shot. I sort of fight for at least my little corner to be a nicer place. (Samantha)

Samantha's experience turned into a spiritual mission to protect others. Other HSPs related similar external orientations, even if they began life focused inwardly. Regardless of when HSPs realize the need to protect themselves, they consider self-protection a priority.

It is hard for HSP's in the work environment. It is still very difficult for me to put up that wall, to shield myself from all those feelings out there and not be affected by other people's feelings. We are labeled as different and sometimes targeted. I mean my last job my manager tormented me. I was the scapegoat. If anything went wrong, it was my fault, which was ludicrous. (Evelyn)

Basically, I think I, because of all the chaos and trauma and things that were going on in my home, I think, I just shut down, and I didn't really know what I wanted. I found that I organized my life in a way that I can stay away from the chaos. (Kurt)

I requested a specific hall because I knew that hall was a lighter hall, an easier hall of people to deal with. These residents didn't require quite as much help, and they weren't as bad as some of the other halls and that protected me from some of the overstimulation. (Hailey)

Overstimulation and boredom are two huge things for me. If I get over stimulated, I feel like the wiring in my body is faulty. (Taylor)

Protecting oneself, in a working environment, where we are not typically able to choose the people we must interact with, leaves us vulnerable to absorbing negative energy, and, its resultant effects, i.e., emotional upset, anxiety at having to see and deal with the individual in the future, a dread of the job itself. The question is, how do we effectively protect ourselves from encountering potentially upsetting individuals or situations? To a certain extent, we are caught between the demands of our positions – which often require extensive interaction with others – and a need to not entirely squash the parts of our sensitivity that makes us unique and whole.

In my survey, 29% of HSPs strongly agreed with the statement "when I am in public, I find that I am easily activated emotionally," 48% agreed.

Let us be clear here, though: there are highly sensitive people at all levels of society and in all manner of careers. HSPs do engage fully and, in fact, are likely the most conscientious employees in a company or organization. This sets up the ironic dichotomy many HSPs feel: they have a deep need to do meaningful work and do it to the best they are capable – which is typically very high – yet certain aspects of the working environment lack in significant ways, leaving HSPs feeling they must protect themselves far and above what other people feel they must do. For some HSPs, the answer is a new job, for others, it's learning to manage the interactions, so they are more tolerable, and for others the best solution is self-employment. As Faith expressed "you cannot expose your vulnerabilities too much because this world will eat you alive!"

In spite of the dozens of self-help books explaining to us how to meditate, how to calm ourselves, and how to eat a balanced diet, we don't spend enough time taking care of our bodies and pay the price for it in ill-health. In as much as we have to learn to manage our strong empathy, we also have to attend to the basics like, what we eat, the amount of exercise we engage in, and the amount of rest we get. These things are critically important to our ability to withstand the barrage of stimulation we face daily. Subtract just the sleep component and one's tolerance is dramatically lowered. Most of us, in the working world, run around sleep deprived and function at much less than our potential. Many of us run out for fast food, at lunch, and, if we had breakfast at all, it was not substantial nor healthy. Our dinner is comprised of an almost equal amount of take-out food as made-at-home if we look at statistics. And exercise, what is that? Who has time, right?

In my survey, 11% of HSPs strongly agreed with the statement "I do not exercise regularly" 30% agreed.

The answer is us, and we can correct all these issues to some extent. What it requires of us as HSPs is a new attitude, one based on a deep commitment to our well-being that can emanate out to others. Highly sensitive people are often the first to notice something being "off," in this case, it is the lifestyle many of us have inherited that is too fast, too unhealthy, too stressful, and just too much.

Is self-care truly no fun or are we simply following society's preprogrammed path for us because it is easier? HSPs are no more immune to societal conditioning than anyone else and are just as subject to the pressures of conformity as anyone else. The difference, for HSPs, is we are typically deeply ethical individuals and will engage in commitments that have deep meaning. Caring for our bodies and minds is, and should be, the first step to serious self-care.

Highly sensitive people – being rather complex individuals – need to think of self-care in a different way. Because we are more deeply affected by stimulation and process it more elaborately – often leading to fatigue and exhaustion – we need to see our bodies as more than just simple organisms. We need to think of ourselves as complex, dynamic systems that are interwoven, that interplay and counterbalance each other. If one system is out of balance, the others cannot possibly hope to function as well as they could. In this view, we respect the complex and intricate nature of our bodily systems laying the groundwork for our further development and flourishing.

A Holistic Approach

An inclusive approach to self-care would include care on many levels:

•Physical – care for the body itself, through careful attention to a diet that works for you, frequent exercise in a form that is sustainable for you, tuning in to the signals your body communicates to you. My survey results indicated a nearly even split between those who exercise and those who do not. Interestingly, nearly 68% of survey respondents indicated they valued "eating right, getting adequate sleep, and staying healthy."

•Emotional – creating and standing by reasonable boundaries, including learning to say no. Doing so ensures, to some extent, that you have protected yourself, where possible. Working on oneself to address issues of dysfunction acquired in childhood or later. This can take the form of attending therapy sessions with a skilled counselor, joining a support group, or researching and reflecting on your own. You are capable of self-healing and know yourself better than anyone.

In my survey, 18% of HSPs strongly agreed with the statement "managing my emotions is very difficult" 42% agreed.

•Social – though many HSPs tend toward the introverted side, we are social creatures and need to be around others at times. At work, it may seem like we get too much of this, but I suggest that view is evaluative of the quality of socialization at work. When we choose who to socialize with, the quality is likely to be much higher, and we may derive greater benefits from the interaction. Socialize in amounts that are appropriate for you and with quality individuals.

•Spiritual – our spiritual selves overarch and encompass all that we are and hope to be. Whether we choose to involve ourselves in a formal religion or engage in a spiritual practice in other ways, it is critically important that we do so. A spiritual practice can be many things: immersing oneself in nature, the practice of yoga, meditation, service to others, or any activity that takes the focus off of oneself and emphasizes awareness and appreciation of a greater reality, while providing grounding of one's energies. My survey additionally indicated that, approximately 67% of HSPs engage in prayer, meditation, or other forms of spiritual communion. Develop and maintain a contemplative practice.

In my survey, 36% of HSPs strongly agreed with the statement "I have some form of spiritual practice" 34% agreed.

The overall societal trend seems to be toward a lessening of emphasis on the community commons with a greater focus on the self. Though that seems to be the mainstream view, it is highly encouraging that many people individually have deviated from this path and placed value once again on interconnection, concern for others, and for less self-centered ways of being. Once our society focused away from the individual and more on the community. Perhaps one of the services HSPs can render to an ill society is to refocus our energies on the good of all.

Self-care practices

A self-care practice is intended to mean any activity engaged in that facilitates a sense of calmness, centeredness, balance, and health, emotionally, physically, and spiritually. A variety of practices emerged from the study including meditation; yoga; connection to nature; motorcycle riding; attention to diet and exercise; setting boundaries; and purposeful selection of friends. These all seemed to be of great importance to participants. Some participants placed a higher value on self-care than they did on career advancement, expressing that their emotional, physical, and spiritual lives have to be in order before they can take on additional demands.

Vitaly, Kirk, and Kurt explain the value of caring for themselves as extremely important in their lives,

Personal growth is something very important to me. It is actually more important than my career at this point...my personal growth is more important to me, so I think career

growth is a violation of myself, that is why I am not into considering career growth as my number one priority. (Vitaly)

I have been able to make connections with practitioners who have helped me from that standpoint. I get massage therapy every two weeks. I think I have been doing that for about fifteen years now, because going back to the internalization of other people's states and my own state and how to handle it, and so forth, I just have to get help working that stuff out of my physical structure. I spend as much time by myself as I can. I need a lot of downtime. By a lot of people's standards, the amount of time I spend by myself is outrageous, but for me, the down time with myself unstructured with no plans, that is how I regenerate. I just have to, in terms of self-care, I need to eat a certain way, and that I give myself every opportunity I can to sort of detach from whatever is going on outside me so the truth that is inside me can have a chance to energize itself and then I can go out again. I walk a mile or two every day. Getting out in nature and getting around animals helps a lot. (Kirk)

Swimming is a huge piece for me. I realize how much I need water in my life just to kind of wash away things that kind of get stuck to me energetically, and because of movement. Swimming is a full body movement, which I think has really been good for me to move everything because I am so tall. It also represents that spaciousness in me, and that really helps. That is self-care. (Kurt)

Vitaly relates his routine for self-care involves physical exercise "I have a routine of four days per week that I do these exercises at whatever the costs. I started this routine the last month and a half." Yoga was reported as a major outlet for self-care by participants. Yoga has been practiced for thousands of years and is primarily intended as a means of attaining a continuous state of peace of mind so one might truly experience oneself and unite with the universal. In Western countries, Hatha yoga is primarily practiced for its physical benefits, but also for its inherent spirituality.

The approach varies by practitioner with some participants reporting deeper involvement, while others focus on the physical aspects. Lucy began practicing yoga by taking classes, soon realizing yoga was her "heart opener." She found yoga allowed her to focus inwardly and "stop being what everybody wanted me to be." Lucy eventually began teaching yoga classes and developed a small business helping others find their true selves. Molly also began practicing yoga, in her words "I started practicing yoga to cope with my features and my panic attacks. I started doing that when I was about eighteen or nineteen and it helps tremendously."

Other participants related that self-care, for them, means learning to be completely self-aware. Kent, for instance, has learned to be more aware of the specific sources of overstimulation and be more flexible in order to avoid them. He is especially triggered by grocery stores, as are many other participants, and if he feels overwhelmed, he simply comes back at another time when it is less crowded. Kent seems to be attuned to his internal states and can manage them based on this awareness. Bruce has also learned to manage his emotional life by what he describes as "post processing" with another person, rather than "taking in those feelings on his own." Adelle has developed a more active approach that includes swimming, walking, reading, and talking with others. She describes self-humor or being able to laugh at oneself as a way of minimizing stressful events as helpful. Adelle emphasized the role of "sharing our gifts with others" as crucial for her.

Olivia incorporates Zumba dance in her set of self-care practices and describes its value in her life:

I do a lot of yoga, I have a meditation practice, now I have a writing practice every day. Interestingly, lately in terms of taking care of my body, I have started taking Zumba dance classes, which usually might not have been something I picked because I was spending so much time writing and thinking and reading. There is something exciting about being playful and dancing to music. It is one of those circumstances when you are not actually interacting with others like in a group and not having to have a fun time, but I think that was always reviving to me when I see these parts of myself that...there is intentionally a contradiction who wants something more to engage with or the part of me that wants to be quiet and sometimes they can even on a given day be in a different place. (Olivia)

Olivia also related to me how she carefully manages her energies "if I am really able to manage my day and my week, then my colleagues never see the part of me that hits the limits." Olivia's responses suggested that setting boundaries are important to HSPs. Boundaries may be limitations one sets that prevent overstimulation or negative stimulation. Joshua's approach is to carefully choose who he spends his time with, thus regulating the stimuli he takes in. He is, however, not an isolationist, rather he has found that as he gets older, his patience for having to deal with negative stimulation is less. This lessening of patience as one ages for negative or overstimulation was a nearly universal sentiment expressed by the HSPs I interviewed. Setting boundaries, in that sense, becomes not only a matter of choosing who to connect with but also a matter of self-preservation.

Taylor related to me a specific protective practice she learned as a young girl,

It was hard, like being so sensitive and knowing things, and people were not always so safe. I feel it was this intuition in myself that kept me and my sister safe. My sister and I used to play this game where we would imagine this healing light. It always started in the solar plexus and then we would emanate it. I remember that would become a meditation habit for me, and it made me feel very safe and warm. I would extend it out to my family, almost like a prayer meditation. I feel like it kept my father safe on the water, it kept my brother safe, it kept my sisters safe. It was just like a game that we played. It was funny because in the last couple of years I have been doing some work with shamans. This is a technique that they used. I think it is amazing that my sister as a child intuitively knew this technique. I believe everything is energy, and we manifest reality with our thoughts. I think that when you do that, it is not only comforting to you like a blanket or a teddy bear, but it is empowering.

In addition to the practices outlined above, HSPs expressed a fundamental need to reappraise how they care for themselves, how they perceive life, and how they should live. This orientation was not in place at a young age for the majority of HSPs, in this study. Rather, they seem to have learned the necessity of self-care after years of career and life stress.

Meditations

Meditations can generally be grouped into three main categories: tranquility, insight, and transcendental or contemplative. The first two meditation exercises below are for tranquility, while the last may be explored for insights. I recommend trying out several differing contemplative practices to find the combination that works for you, given your specific background and needs. The development of a contemplative practice should be a top priority for any HSP that wishes to calm and focus the mind or gain greater awareness into the nature of our being and potentialities. I also recommend reading *The Experience of Meditation*, by Jonathan Schear.

1.   *Quick Centering Meditation* – find a quiet place where you can sit. Sit with feet flat on the floor, hands in a comfortable position. Close your eyes and focus only on your breathing. Resist the urge to allow your mind to run away with itself (and it likely will). Instead, focus as you breath in, noting your lungs expanding, your chest filling. Breath in deeply, hold for a second at the end and allow it to escape slowly and naturally. Focus on your exhale, your chest falling, your body doing exactly what is natural for it to. Be in this place of simply breathing and not allowing the cares of the world to invade for at least 3 minutes. At the end when you feel ready to allow your eyes to open. From this still, quiet place you have reached reenter the world knowing you can come back to this place at any time.

2.   *Walking meditation* – notice your body before beginning to move, how it stands upright and constantly adjusts muscles, tendons, and your center of gravity just to stay upright. As you begin to walk notice your feet how your heel feels as it strikes the ground then the balls of your feet. Next, notice how your legs lift and move on each step, how your body maintains its momentum and balance as we move forward. Notice your calves, your thighs as they flex and lift. Notice your breath as you breathe in and out on each step. Notice how your body adjusts to what you are asking of it. Focus on being in your body and being in the world. When you balance the inner and outer, you may find that you reach a point of stillness, calm and quiet, even in movement. Go with this feeling and simply be in it for a period. As you reach a natural ending point for your walk,

slowly decrease your speed, but do not stop suddenly. Spend a moment just calmly existing in that still place before you reenter the demands of your life knowing that you can walk anytime and be in this place of calm and stillness within a few minutes.

3.   *Guided meditations* – many western HSPs might find it quite difficult to meditate because they have been conditioned by their societies to continually tolerate some level of stimulation, even in a quiet environment.   Many may find guided meditations very helpful because it more closely approximates prior conditioning.   In a guided meditation, you would typically sit quietly while listening to a speaker lead you through a series of breathing exercises designed to calm you, attune you to your bodily processes and rhythms, and perhaps invoke a particular intent, such as suggesting the individuals in the group enter the next activity with great openness and awareness.   At other times, the intent may be to simply calm the mind, lessen anxiety, or allow us to enter a contemplative space for a period of time.   Guided meditations are available online through web sites like YouTube, the UCLA's Mindful Aware Research Center (short online meditations), and audiodharma.org.

Advice for HSPs

Q: I feel stressed so much of the time from work, family, and other demands. How can I reduce my stress levels?

A: There are many ways to reduce one's stress levels from exercise to activities that effectively allow you to "escape," even for a short while like going to the beach, park, or woods. At work, simply taking a short walk will do wonders for your emotional well-being and health.   We each need our daily quota of fresh air and sunshine, and even this simple need is overlooked by many people. Get out and move, your body is designed to be in motion most of the time! Adjust your diet, get enough sleep, and find ways to commune with nature or otherwise take the focus off yourself and onto a larger appreciation of the positive sides of life. If these things do not exist in your workplace start a walking group on breaks, it will catch on.

Q: I am not interested in organized religions, but still have a strong spiritual side. How can I indulge this?

A: Being out in nature is one of the best avenues to connecting with the infinite. Serving others is another way to remove the focus from yourself and develop compassion. At work, it is important to be able to self-soothe and function from a quiet, still center. Being a sensitive, creative, deep-feeling and thinking individual is hard in noisy, demanding workplaces, but it is still possible to embody the essence of who you are and be a strong example to others through your quiet, inner strength.

Chapter 5

The inner depths

"The monotony and solitude of a quiet life stimulates the creative mind." Albert Einstein

The defining aspect of sensory processing sensitivity, for many people, is the tendency toward overstimulation in certain situations, but confining what it means to be a highly sensitive person to the sensory realm only is to deny the complexity and beauty inherent in our beings and what we embody. True, most of us do have issues with sensory overwhelm, but many have found ways to cope and manage to minimize the impact. Most male HSPs, in fact, seem to have marginalized the sensory overwhelm tendency and focus on the emotional aspect, which is an absolute core feature of sensory processing sensitivity. For males, it is generally socially unacceptable to appear to be emotional or overwhelmed, in any circumstance. Thus, many learn to desensitize themselves or learn to lessen their reactivity. Indeed, no two HSPs are alike: one may abhor bright lights, while another needs strong daylight. Some HSPs are bothered by smells, noises, or crowded conditions, while others have no such issues. The important point here is that highly sensitive people are not a homogenous group of individuals, beyond the four main characteristics of sensory processing sensitivity, which can be thought of using the DOES acronym.

- Depth of processing, of all stimulation

- Overstimulation, in certain circumstances

- Emotional responsiveness and high empathy

- Sensitivity to subtle stimuli

Highly sensitive people are deeply complex individuals, who live in a state of heightened sensory awareness. They do not possess super senses in any way, rather, the way stimulation is processed in the brain is more elaborate. In this chapter, let us look at some examples that illustrate the inner depths of the highly sensitive person.

The sensory realm

Highly sensitive people are subject to a barrage of sensory stimulation daily that may be overwhelming and counterproductive in a work environment. Others may not experience the same sensitivities and may not take the person seriously or may tune out the requests. Almost three-quarters of the HSPs, in my survey, strongly agreed concerning overstimulation issues. Let us look at a few quotes from HSPs describing what it is like to feel overstimulated at work:

It was the constant stimulation, the people running around in back of me doing things...the first time anybody ever said anything to me about looking anxious was when I couldn't find the button I needed to push to order their meal, and I was shaking and that person told me "it's ok, calm down." And I didn't even realize it, they saw it, but I didn't know I was doing it, so I guess to them I was overanxious, but I was very overstimulated...I felt so tired and so overwhelmed...it was, it was just call lights going off, sounds overhead, griping at each other, patients crying out in pain. I had a lady who was a double amputee in a lot of pain. (Hailey)

In my survey, 72% of HSPs strongly agreed with the statement "I feel distracted, overstimulated by bright lights, strong smells, crowded office arrangements, or uncomfortable temperatures," 24% agreed.

If there was just kind of a constant busy day, so constantly dealing with people and, say, that goes on for a period of three hours. I am so frazzled when I am done, that I kind of just completely zone out and not talk to anyone for an extended period of time. (Molly)

I cannot stand loud talking. If I am on a train and hear loud talking, I literally get out and go to another train. It just drives me nuts how loud people are talking. I cannot take it when I am on a train. When I am on a bus, I can tolerate it, you know, if I ask them to quiet down, they give me a hard time about it. Chewing, I cannot stand chewing. People who chew with their mouth open just bugs me. It sounds like smacking, you know, chomp, chomp, chomp. There is a guy at work now that does it and I say, "uh hum" and I wrote down how many times a day he did it. I asked him about it, and he said it was a new thing, it went on for a month, but he has quieted down, so everything is okay, but he was driving me nuts. I go around asking people around him if they hear him, and they say, yeah, so no one speaks out...when people are eating chips out of the bag, and it crinkles, they eat one chip at a time, and they go back in the bag and it sounds like, you know, it jars my ears. It just irritates the hell out of me. I just usually walk away and take a walk or something. (Kent)

The stimulation that comes into a nurse's daily life in a hospital is you just wouldn't believe, you cannot imagine it, for instance, you are standing there at the nurse's server (that is the door outside the patient's room) you are carrying a Netcom phone, which hourly beeps to give you instructions to do something that you can't and you are not wanting to do anyway, but they decided that you need to be reminded anyway so the phone goes off. The phone is ringing, and the patient's family comes out and talks to you, and there is a big sweeper or shampooer shampooing the rug all the way up and down several times behind your back, and there are announcements overhead at the same time then the fire alarm drill goes off, ding, ding, ding, ding. I mean it is just sometimes, I just have to stand there plant my feet and stare and just take it moment by moment until it goes away if I cannot get out of it at the moment...the stimulation as a hospital nurse is immense. (Julia)

Julia's very poignant description of too much stimulation from too many directions was common in my study, and one begins to understand the human toll – in terms of stress – that are part and parcel of many jobs. Some HSPs learn to desensitize themselves to certain stimuli or enter states of alienation, as Julia seems to be describing above. In any case, the important takeaway is the crucial importance that self-care plays in providing us with the necessary recuperation and rest to remain functional in our daily lives. For those who are unable to change careers or positions, the need for self-care is even greater.

How Do I Deal with Overstimulation?

For the HSPs who consistently experience overstimulation as an issue, the key to managing it is developing and maintaining an awareness of the tendency. When we know that certain noises, smells, or irritants are present, we can work to minimize their impact on our immediate and future well-being.

The obvious first step is to let others know something is amiss. HSPs usually notice these issues first and should not feel bad about requesting a comfortable working environment where possible. Others may be experiencing the same thing but may not have spoken up yet. The other obvious step – especially if you are in a position where you can control environmental factors – is simply to do so. If the lights are too bright, try turning off or dimming one or more, so the lighting is more comfortable. If there are irritating noises, shut a door or otherwise limit their impact. These simple steps may help with controlling some issues of overstimulation, but, in some workplace environments, there are ever-present sensory irritants that simply go along with the job.

I have worked in jobs that exposed me to all of nature's elements, hot, cold, rain, snow, and everything in between. I have also worked in interior environments that were noisy, too bright (fluorescent lighting), too hot, too crowded, and totally out of sync with my own bodily rhythms (night shift). Through it all one has to find ways to keep the mind calm, the body healthy, and, as reasonably comfortable as is possible at any given moment, and to do so in a sustainable way that allows one to get through each work week. This might sound somewhat harsh, but the reality is not all of us will be able to change our lives to such an extent that we find the perfect environment. In those cases, being able to sustainably endure is the focus.

The Just-Right Bright Side of a HSP's Sensory World

The tendency for many HSPs to become overstimulated by certain sensory sensations is undeniable but let us remember the flipside: HSPs also have a deeper capacity for enjoyment of sensory experiences of all types! The HSP who is exposed and surrounded by stimulation they choose may truly be in sensory heaven and perform at the top of their game.

Creativity

Are creative people highly sensitive? The association has long been implied due to our temperament, but until now there has not been an empirical link. One of the most frequently mentioned words by participants in the initial study was creativity. HSPs, by virtue of their ability to notice subtleties before others, greater capacity for aesthetic enjoyment, complexity of mind, and sense of curiosity are innately predisposed toward creativity.1 In the first study, approximately 75% of participants described themselves as "creative." By creative, I imply a broader definition than commonly expressed as producing an end product. Barron defined creativity as "the ability to respond adaptively to the need for new ways of being...the ability to bring something new into existence."2 Barron elucidated a common core of characteristics that appear consistently across fields: independence of judgment; a preference for complexity; a strong desire to create; a deep motivation or drive--which Barron called the cosmological motive--to create one's own universe of meaning, personally defined; lots of personal troubles linked to an intense sensibility; a strongly intuitive nature; and patience or endurance, persistence, and basic optimism in the face of difficulty.2

Pairing Barron's encapsulation2 with Csikszentmihalyi's contention that "the one word that makes creative people different is complexity" referring to an ability to express "the full range of traits that are potentially present in the human repertoire"3 and Storr's view that the "one feature of creative people is their capacity for change and development...linked to their openness to their own feelings and emotions and also to impressions and new ideas from outside" I determined, utilizing the aforementioned definition, that over 90 percent of participants were likely creative. Of the remaining 10 percent it is likely their issues with anxiety, fear, and depression inhibit any significant development of creativity.

A further link between creativity and HSPs was established in my second study when 86% of HSPs taking the survey agreed or strongly agreed with the statement "I am a creative person." Pressing deeper, I posed the statement "I do not like to create new things." In this instance, 85% of HSPs who responded either disagreed or strongly disagreed. Relating creativity to work, I next offered the statement "I prefer work that engages my creative capacities deeply." Of the HSPs who responded, 78% agreed or strongly agreed. These two studies represent the first time HSPs and creativity have been linked together. What do I surmise from this strong link? I think it is reasonable to say that most HSPs are creative, but not all creative people are HSPs. Much more research needs to be done to understand better how to envision creativity as HSPs, use it in the workplace, and in our communities. More research also needs to be conducted comparing creativity in HSPs and non-HSPs to establish a clearer representation of actual percentages in the total population.

Creative engagement.

The HSPs, in the initial study, expressed a need for creative engagement on many levels. Linda related "I also had some interest in architecture and just drawing. I am a visual thinker and a systems thinker, so things related to that. I also like dealing with materials, so dealing with materials or other things that you can get your hands into." Linda's preference is for a working environment where her creativity is "encouraged and utilized." Claire emphasized that creative engagement, for her, means more than simply being viewed as a "design monkey." In her view, creative engagement is about the freedom and autonomy to engage her curiosity in meaningful ways that honors and builds on all of her skills and abilities that matters,

I like the type of graphic design where I could combine my painting with graphic design, so a lot of the books that I

made I used original paintings and scanned them in and used them as part of the book. That was a really great experience. I had that full control over what I was designing and all the content and was able to research what I wanted to do. That was great. (Claire)

The need for a certain degree of creative control seemed to be important to many HSPs. Autonomy of action was another major element that participants valued. Though most participants stated that they liked to work in quiet environment at times, or alone, they also articulated a need to collaborate in small groups. Finally, several HSPs described a token desire for creativity on the part of organizations or companies they worked for. Linda related how in several of her positions, as she was close to leaving each position, her supervisor would tell her they "wanted creativity, but not that much."

Love of learning

Highly sensitive people are the deep, reflective segment of our species, the ones who are naturally predisposed toward a love of learning. Our innate ability to notice subtleties before others enables us to be the first to discover something new and interesting. The penchant for observing aids this process by allowing for the gathering of extensive information utilizing our senses. This natural love of learning was reflected in the HSPs I interviewed.

I like taking pictures a lot. I was always into writing. That was always kind of my thing. I was into reading and writing, and I still am…I think I always wanted to be a writer. I gradually wanted to become a teacher as well; my whole family is a family of teachers. (Colleen)

I am not only sitting in my house, and I go on trips, and I am very curious. I try to find the meaning about things, and I read a lot, and I study a lot…I do not think my curiosity will stop. I read about things, and I am so curious... In childhood, I always had to have something to study. (Astrid)

I wrote a play. I acted it out. I wrote it. I did that last year. I never wrote a play in my life. I took writing classes, playwriting classes at a place in town. I took photography. I have taken dancing. I was in taekwondo for a while. (Kent)

In my survey, 52% of HSPs strongly agreed with the statement "Learning new things is important to me in my career" a further 36% agreed.

I think that the internet and ability to do online classes is just the greatest thing ever for me. I love it! I am so happy that I do have so much to do now...I have always been incredibly curious about everything. (Ava)

The same attitude toward learning applies in the workplace, with one interesting divergence: HSPs from unsupportive backgrounds described a level of anxiety related to uncertainty regarding employer expectations, when something new is introduced. Some anxiety is to be expected, but if it becomes paralyzing or crippling opportunities, may be lost along with the realization of personal potential. One of the strategies I have always used is to take notes when learning a new task with detailed step-by-step procedures, where appropriate. At the least, this approach offers the confidence that you will be following an agreed upon procedure, at a minimal level. Later refinements may occur, as one repeats certain procedures, and learns better ways of accomplishing the task or goal. Everyone will have a slightly different way that will ease your anxiety on the job when learning a new task. Find and develop those to enhance your sense of self-confidence. Remember, HSPs are highly conscientious individuals who have a need to do a job well.

Visual-spatial learning style

One aspect of learning we often overlook, but which deserves our attention here, is learning style. HSPs being predisposed toward creativity due to their ability to notice subtle details before others, ease of entering altered states of consciousness, and tolerance for ambiguity, learn in a different way than most of the rest of society, for whom our schools have constructed a linear learning style, based on strict reproductive learning. HSPs may prefer a more visual mode of learning, one that makes connections intuitively through different neural pathways. For this reason, many HSPs may need to work out concepts in a way more suited to their individual learning style.

Not all HSPs are visual learners. HSPs are psychologically and emotionally androgynous individuals who are able to encompass a broader range of learning styles than may be prevalent in the rest of the population; however, I feel that awareness of one's learning style/s may help as we indulge our need to explore and learn.

For employers, there may be a lesson here: employees who are HSPs, may be more visually oriented when learning a new activity or may encompass more than one learning style. What does this mean for you? It may mean those individuals are predisposed toward thinking about problems in a different way. The bonus for you (and the opportunity) is new solutions to problems may arise if you encourage employees to learn and work in ways that are appropriate for them. This natural "spinning of the wheels" speaks to a complex and rich inner life inherent in HSPs.

Complexity of thought

Highly sensitive people process thoughts more deeply than do others. This means they prefer to think before acting, to consider the possibilities before choosing the best option.   In a workplace environment, this can be a tremendous asset. Reflective individuals with a capacity to envision more than the current problem, save money in the long run by anticipating potential problems before they arise. Helping HSPs make the most of this innate capacity offers employers a great entry point for understanding HSPs. Olivia describes her propensities here:

I realized that I am very contemplative. I like a lot of my work to be big picture. I like to be reflecting on things. I am not a big doer, I mean, I am not the person who can set up big meetings and stuff like, let's get packing or like, let's not sit around and talk about ideas, let's get to work... I realize that I am much more comfortable in the world of ideas when I am in the world. In the world of action, I have no reflection whatsoever. If I must pick one or the other, I want to be in the world of contemplation, thinking, and ideas.

In my survey, 48% of HSPs strongly disagreed with the statement "I do not prefer for things to be well thought out" a further 33% disagreed.

The emphasis on "big picture" thinking was offset by other reports of liking highly detailed work, such as Seth, "I was a tinkerer. I loved to take things apart and see how they worked and figure things out and build things. I was always really good with math and science." The majority of HSPs, in the initial study, reported a strong dislike for math, while a minority reported a strong liking for math and science. Seth's description of desiring to understand the interrelationships between components inside electrical devices echoed the theme of complexity of thought, albeit in a more focused manner. Evelyn related how complexity of thought can also be an unwanted asset in a work situation:

It's the old canary in the coal mine phenomenon where there is dysfunction in a work situation, somehow I would get involved, either, it will be directed at me, and I was intelligent enough to see what was going on and the dysfunction under the surface. Unfortunately, most of the places I have worked they really are not interested in that. It can be useful information, or it can be the idea that we do not want to deal with the fact that we could be contributing to or causing the problem.

The "canary in the coal mine" phrase was used repetitively by many HSPs, in the initial study, to describe how they often feel while at work. Being naturally predisposed toward the big picture and long-term thinking privileges one with knowing what may happen if a given course is taken or not altered. Many HSPs, however, did not report that this ability was valued by employers or understood, as in the quote.

With this ability to think in complex terms, a number of HSPs reported giftedness in school or graduating from college with high honors. In Linda's case, her giftedness translated into academic achievement with a bachelor's degree in mechanical engineering, a master's in nutrition and a master's in divinity. In other cases, recognition of early giftedness did not necessarily translate to career success regarding a linear trajectory of increasingly responsible and rewarding positions. Instead, in the cases of Faith and Lucy, their natural complexity of thought seems to have entailed a longer journey of self-discovery, as Faith relates:

I had never, to this day, known what I wanted to do when I grow up. I still don't know...I was so confused that my folks actually sent me to a psychologist that was working with the people out at my Dad's place and they had me do some vocational testing...I really felt underutilized all of my life.

Lucy's work experiences eventually led her to self-employment where she was able to blend her interests in teaching yoga and consulting with other HSPs on finding their authentic selves and living in a manner that acknowledges complexity. This complexity of thought is a key component that influences the way HSPs in experience careers.

Dislike of Superficiality

Knowing that HSPs are deeply reflective individuals, it may not come as a total surprise that they also tend to dislike superficiality, in all its forms. This does not mean they are loners; indeed some 30% of HSPs are extraverts, but it does mean they value time and space to think. Some 97%, of my survey respondents, either strongly agreed or agreed with the following statement "I require time and space to think." How does this play out in the workplace where it may be noisy or busy with chatter? Many HSPs have probably already developed defense mechanisms that allow to them to survive in such environments, or they have already moved on. For those who may be new to a position, adjusting to, not only background noise, but interpersonal chatter may be distracting, even irritating. Anything HSPs must focus on drains their energy leaving them with less to give to the job.

In my survey, 21% of HSPs strongly agreed with the statement "I prefer for things to have a definite outcome" a further 46% agreed.

For the HSP, you might think "Yes, that's me! I do not like superficial small talk and would rather engage people in deeper conversations and on a one-on-one basis!" Does this mean you are a loner who is antisocial or grumpy? Not at all! You simply prefer your conversations to have content, meaning, and some level of significance because small talk feels superficial and, thus negatively stimulating. This drain on your energy budget can be very detrimental. There are times, however, when an HSP should engage others in pleasant small talk. Why? The reason is, that it is through small talk that people get a chance to know you and appreciate your wonderful depth! In time, you may find others seeking you out because they know you have a complexity of mind and creativity. These are not bad things to be known for.

Advice for HSPs

Q: How can I approach my manager about things that really cause me to feel overstimulated like the bright lights, sudden noises, temperatures too high or low without them thinking I am a complainer?

A: Always approach managers and supervisors from an efficiency and productivity standpoint. They understand the bottom line, which is if you are too hot or cold or have headaches from the lights you cannot get your work done the way they expect. Some managers will get this, some will not, but always come at it from a strengths perspective "Boy, I could really get this project done sooner if I wasn't freezing!"

Q: I prefer to think things through carefully before presenting options, but at work, I am often expected to deliver plans that are less than ready. How can I explain that my plans are better?

A: HSPs are very good at seeing the complexity of theoretical situations noting potential pitfalls and developing options, but that takes time, and many businesses operate on a good-enough basis. You can certainly try explaining to your bosses that long-range planning is better, but if they are not buying it now, they may not be very receptive. One strategy you may use is to develop the rough bones of a few options and present those. While others are debating the merits, you continue to work out the details. Being able to quickly present even a rough sketch of a viable alternative may help your bosses view you as an asset and be more willing in the long run to give you the latitude you need.

Q: At work, I am often flooded with emails that are unclear in their language. How can I improve the clarity of my communications?

A: Not everyone is a verbal learner. Many HSPs are to a high degree visual learner and understand best by graphic representations of a process or plan. I suggest utilizing visual graphics to your advantage wherever you can to communicate your points. Over 90% of the information we take in comes in through our eyes and workplace communications are moving more toward a visual modality.

Chapter 6

High Sensation-Seeking HSPs

"Yeah, I'm a thrill seeker, but Crikey, education's the most important thing." ~Steve Irwin

Roughly 30% of HSPs have a separate personality trait known as sensation seeking. Sensation seeking is a personality trait that has been linked to one or more dopamine uptake genes, thus, like sensory processing sensitivity, it is largely genetic with about 57 percent heritability.1 The interplay between these two traits is quite a fascinating one because they are nearly dichotomous. Sensory processing sensitivity is marked by deep processing in the brain, high empathy, tendencies toward overstimulation, and sensitivity to subtleties, while sensation-seeking has four main components:

- Adventure or thrill-seeking.

- Experience or novelty seeking

- Disinhibition

- Susceptibility toward boredom

Let us unpack each of these aspects just a little then we will relate them to high sensitivity. *Thrill and adventure-seeking* is what we might think of when we hear the term sensation seeker and, for many, it does mean a love of sensation through physical thrills. This may be in any activity where one might experience a rush or strong sensation during the adventure, like rock climbing, hang gliding, racing motorcycles, etc. *Experience or novelty seeking* is searching out new experiences just for the sake of having the experience, the newness. Individuals who are strong in this aspect crave novelty. *Disinhibition* is a willingness, or uninhibitedness, to go outside normal bounds in search of the thrill or experience. Think of Mardi Gras or New Year's Eve, for instance, when many people regularly suspend their normal behaviors as they participate in festivities. Disinhibition is a willingness to enter a different experience, even if it means stepping outside the lines that society has established as norms of behavior. Lastly, *susceptibility toward boredom* is a tendency to find repetition and routine boring. For sensation seekers, boredom may be a major issue.

Each of these items do not sound severe individually, but when we consider that an HSP normally may prefer to observe before acting, being a sensation seeker, which may be more accurately thought of like the approach part of the approach/observe paradigm, means one feels a simultaneous push and pull to approach and observe. In real terms, this means an HSP who is also a sensation seeker, feels a strong need for variety, novelty, new experiences, and possibly physical thrills with a commensurate restraining impulse. In all cases, it seems that the sensation seeker is mostly concerned with the intensity of the experience, not the risk itself. HSS/HSPs love the feeling of novelty, the rush of doing something dangerous, exciting, even naughty. The counterbalancing mechanism is high sensitivity. HSS/HSPs who seek thrills tend to do so with caution. They do not tend to take unnecessary risks.

How does being a sensation-seeking HSP impact career?

In several ways. HSS/HSPs may embody one or more of the four factors already detailed. Each of those aspects of sensation seeking, mingled with sensitivity, may make finding work that supplies enough novelty, new experiences, room for growth, and interest quite difficult depending on one's level of self-awareness from an early age, the area where one resides, and overall integration of sensation seeking with sensitivity. One of the major factors in sensation seeking is boredom. Boredom is also a serious issue for HSPs.4 To better understand how HSS/HSPs experience boredom, let us look at a few experiences.

Threat of boredom

Boredom is my worst enemy...if there was a job that I do that is boring, I quit. I was working at a grocery store and lasted three hours. They wanted me to bag groceries over and over until I got it right. I was like, I got it right the second time, because I go to the grocery store, and I bag my groceries anyways. I have had these jobs where I am like, if I am bored, I just go to them and say, I am so sorry, sometimes I would say I was offered another job, but if it is like, boredom, I can't do it. I do not know what I would do if I were bored. I cannot do the same thing; it is my worst enemy. (Taylor)

The constraint of the work and the boredom...there was nothing exciting to do; I was restless. (Adelle)

Boredom for an HSS/HSP may be related to a task that is repetitious and uninteresting, or it may be due to simply being around boring individuals (yes, they do exist!). In a workplace setting, we typically do not have control over who we spend our workday with and may experience the constraint Adelle spoke of, even to the point of claustrophobia, the feeling of needing to get away. This may lead many HSS/HSPs to leave a job.

In my survey, 19% of HSPs strongly agreed with the statement "I am easily bored." a further 26% agreed.

Think of it this way: many HSS/HSPs are very creative individuals who need stimulation and variety. Working in a job where these very basic requirements are not met is a sort of slow torture that can go on as long as the person is willing or able to tolerate it. There is a danger here: allowing oneself to intentionally work beneath one's abilities and strengths can lead to alienation and detachment. When one is resigned to standing in a stream of negativity, there can be no growth or feelings of satisfaction. One either gives up or makes a break for it regardless of the consequences.

I am not suggesting that you run for the hills any time you are bored on the job, but if you are in a situation where it obviously does not fit you well, I do recommend planning your "escape" by searching for more suitable work while you are still employed. Leaving a job before having other employment can result in some obvious negative ramifications. I have walked off a job only one time but have quit others with no viable plan. As HSS/HSPs, we not only need to remain within a range of optimal stimulation, we also must contend with the challenges of being highly sensitive. Balancing the two is entirely possible, but it requires a high level of self-awareness and attentiveness to both competing sides. Though boredom may be a significant factor for many HSS/HSPs, there is another aspect of sensation seeking that seems to overlap well with sensitivity: a sense of curiosity.

Curiosity/Exploring

Highly sensitive people by nature are curious individuals who like to investigate complexities and explore possibilities. Rarely, do HSPs prefer extremes of black and white. For sensation seeking HSPs, curiosity is also prominent for those who seek new experiences and novelty. Bruce stated, "I was just kind of seeking adventure and growing up outside and trying to find new places to go. I explored the neighborhood a lot on my bike and just was always looking for adventure." For HSS/HSPs, high in this aspect, the world is full of interesting people, places, and things waiting to be explored. We would usually rather explore a new place than go to a familiar place.

Need for short-term projects

The sensation seeking HSPs, in my initial study, expressed their need to work more on a project basis, with definite ending dates and new projects always on the horizon, than for repetitive, stable, and never-ending projects. Here, Bruce articulates his position on being a sensation seeking HSP,

It is very interesting. Every day is different. I think that is what it comes down to for me, is that I really listen to myself and ask what kind of energy I have today. Some days, I have a lot of energy and can do a lot, but other days if I have been through a stressful situation the day before, I need to do self-care, so the balance is really tricky, but I appreciate the framework now...because I was all over the place, but, now, I feel like I have been able to find a balance. I do appreciate that it does help being a high sensation-seeker, it does give me the motivation to be creative and to kind of work through things when I need it. There is an advantage to it. (Bruce)

Bruce also denoted a need to balance his sensation-seeking side with his highly sensitive side,

I find that I am the most balanced than I have been earlier in my life. I think my high sensation kind of dominated more because that is how I got acceptance from other people, but now I am really embracing my sensitive side, so I find that is

what is coming out.

Joshua's experience was different. He worked as a psychodrama therapist, only finding a need for balance after completely burning himself out. He stated:

It was high action and a lot of activity. Everything is about spontaneity and creativity, and those are two traits that I wanted to develop in myself. Even as I was directing, I was developing that because, in directing you have to be spontaneous and very creative in the moment, and all the time under pressure. I like that. It is kind of like running down the street with your hair on fire. It was just; it made me feel powerful....I couldn't handle doing what people wanted me to do...what I do realize is I was burning out the whole time...I was getting stressed, pretty stressed and I was working hard, and I started feeling that. I was doing groups in psychiatric hospitals, and it was becoming uncreative to me. It was just doing the same things repeatedly. I got tired of it and bored. I wanted to get into a more creative aspect of psychodrama and then the mechanical aspect of it, and so I think, clinical psychodrama bored me...It finally burned me out. (Joshua)

As with all things, there are complexities and the need to explore may be tempered at times with a need to rest or simply observe.

Chouko described her experiences:

I am high sensation-seeking, but I cannot stay too long in one place that is why I did not get a full-time job. I must move around. One job is not enough...Yes, different, like teaching, psychotherapy, and housewife. I teach, I help my husband's job...he is a lot of things to me or I get bored...people tell me to concentrate on researcher, but I cannot. I cannot do this as a full-time, though, because I get bored... so I want to do something I can finish. I like making things. I make bags and stuff. I mean sewing too...I want to try something new if it looks very interesting, but at the same time, I need to withdraw it. I need time...Always, I am fighting with it.

As part of the survey, I included a sensation seeking test that provided some interesting insights into how sensitivity seems to overlap with sensation seeking. I was not able to differentiate between the participants who were HSPs and HSS/HSPs (perhaps in another study), but the responses to certain questions tell a tale of shared curiosity and an exploratory nature. Consider the following responses:

If it were safe, I would like to take a drug that would cause me to have strange, new experiences. Approximately 58% disagreed or strongly disagreed, while almost 30% agreed or strongly agreed. This seems to reinforce the 30% of HSPs as sensation seekers and conversely reinforce how strongly non-HSS/HSPs might react to such a question.

If I see something unusual, I will go out of my way to check it out. Approximately 64% agreed or strongly agreed. This result seems to indicate that sensation seekers and highly sensitive people tend to experience a similar sense of curiosity and need to explore.

I like to explore a new area. Approximately 73% agreed or strongly agreed.

I have a need to work on new projects. Approximately 65% agreed or strongly agreed.

This need to explore, learn, and grow seems to be a major asset in the working world, but many HSPs reported that it's quite the opposite with many positions stifling their curiosity and providing few, if any, opportunities for growth and development. For the sensation seeking HSP, any stifling of innate drive to explore and learn may lead to unacceptable boredom. Many report leaving positions because the boredom and lack of opportunities created intolerable feelings of frustration or depression. For the sensation seeking HSP, this propensity may lead to burnout that can affect one's psychological and physical health. There is no stronger advice I can give for the sensation-seeking HSP than that self-care is a must!

Self-Care

The sensation seeking HSP is a bit more complex than the normal HSP, in that they have the additional drive to seek out novelty, avoid boredom, and indulge in a certain amount of thrill seeking or, potentially, disinhibition. Sensation seeking tends to decline somewhat with age, but the propensity for some aspects will likely remain. This tug of war between caution (on the part of the highly sensitive side) and advancing (on the sensation seeking side) may prove exhausting if the two are not well balanced. One cannot continually thrill seek while ignoring the cautious and sensitive side without squashing it. In theory, if a sensation seeking HSP learns to balance the two traits it is the best of both worlds, with the drive to advance coupled with a commiserate reflective capacity tempering impulsivity. However, the drain on one's energy may be immense, and the need to approach self-care with a new attitude cannot be overstated.

Self-care, for the sensation-seeking HSP, must be so integrated with one's way of being that the necessary actions become fluid and unforced with the same dedication some practice their religions. In essence, self-care becomes the spiritual practice for the sensation-seeking HSP, but unforced. What I am suggesting is more in line with the Tao where one views oneself moving through life as if made of water, flowing with it instead of forcing and controlling. In that sense, self-care moves beyond a "practice," which implies conscious effort and more to a way of being that simply "is."

Reaching a point where self-care is as fluid and natural, as described above, takes some time, but too many of us wait until our health has already failed, and we are exhausted by the demands of life. There is no better time to begin developing a serious self-care mindset than now. Begin it now and carry forward with it as naturally as your breath.

Sensation seeking HSPs are a unique subgroup within the HSP population (some 30%), with a twin need for approaching and observing. Harnessed with finesse, the two traits can be a fantastic combination. Careers that sensation seeking HSPs would do well in are numerous. The ones they would not likely not do well in are those with too much repetition, little variety in the work, long-term projects, and those that are unable to keep them at their optimal level of arousal. Other than that, the potential is unlimited!

Advice for sensation seeking HSPs

Q: I find it more acceptable to be the sensation seeker than the HSP, but that means I am constantly doing things to please other people. How do I just be myself?

A: First, stop worrying about pleasing other people or what they will think of you if you say no. Being who you are, even if that means you occasionally say no to an adventure or overstimulating event, simply means you are doing what you need to in order to take good care of yourself. It is perhaps more acceptable to be a sensation seeker, at least better understood, than to be highly sensitive, but to embody both traits means we must honor and respect the gifts and responsibilities of embodying both equally. Learning to do this takes time. Forgive yourself for when you have to say no and be compassionate with other's needs as well.

Q: I go from job to job out of boredom. It has been hard because I find myself interested in a new position for a few weeks then it turns into a routine and becomes boring. I feel myself become emotionally depressed and can feel it in my bones. What can I do, I feel so out of step with everyone else?

A: You are out of step with everyone else. Your needs are more complex because you are a more complex person! As a sensation seeking HSP, it is likely you will have to view a career in a different light. One where you are more project based and possibly one with less stability than one might like. My advice is to find at least one thing you can do that brings in a significant percentage of your monthly income, even if it is somewhat routine and boring, and work on other projects to balance out the rest. Keep searching for new projects, keep networking and building relationships, and, above all else, keep up your self-care.

Q: Sometimes I do things that qualify me as disinhibited and I often feel like what I am about to do is risky, but do it anyway, which has gotten me in trouble in many ways. What can I do?

A: Sensation seekers often underestimate the level of risk in their activities, especially the thrill and adventure seekers. There can be legal, financial, and personal ramifications for each. Having a highly sensitive side means you have a natural capacity to think ahead and better estimate the risk.   Learn to listen to that voice urging caution and reflection before plunging ahead.   You will avoid much trouble later!

Q: I feel like I do not know who I am with the two personality traits. The sensation seeker is always ready to go, while the highly sensitive side is more observant and more low-key. How can I find out who I am?

A: Assuming you are a younger person, that self-knowledge will come in time to an extent, but you must make an effort to read and learn all you can about both traits so you are fully aware of your propensities and can balance both traits in your actions.   Sensation seeking tends to decline somewhat as we age and you may find yourself becoming more reflective and contemplative as you get older.   None of us are static; we just do not easily acknowledge it.

Chapter 7

The Sociological Context

"We seldom realize, for example, that our most private thoughts and emotions are not actually our own. For we think in terms of languages and images which we did not invent, but which were given to us by our society." ~Alan Watts

The "Big Picture"

Each society has its own specific characteristics within which individuals live and act. Sociologist C. Wright Mills explained that "the sociological perspective enables us to grasp the connection between history and biography." By history, Mills was referring to the collection of specific events that form and shape a society's ideas about various aspects of life like beliefs, rules, and roles. By biography, Mills meant our specific experiences within the society that produce an orientation toward life. Our location in a society largely determines what we do and how we think.

Even though we may believe that we are each thinking and acting on our own, every action we take is centered in a perspective toward life that is rooted in a number of sociological factors including culture, social class, and gender. Consequently, the picture of complexity within which HSPs live and work becomes no more apparent than in the sociological context. In this chapter, we will examine the above categories plus attempt to unpack an overall context of HSPs in society.

Culture

"Culture is made up of the totality of knowledge, skills, rules,

standards, prohibitions, strategies, beliefs, ideas, values, and myths passed from generation to generation and reproduced in each individual, which control the existence of the society and maintain psychological and social complexity. There is no human society, either archaic or modern, without a culture, but every culture is singular." Edgar Morin

First, let us define culture as made up of material and non-material aspects. In the material world, culture is art, buildings, machines, hairstyles, clothing, jewelry, weapons, even eating utensils. Non-material culture is a group's way of thinking (including its values, beliefs, and assumptions) and doing (its common patterns of behavior, including language, gestures, and other forms of interaction). There is nothing inherently natural about culture. It is completely arbitrary as to whether one is "right" in wearing short shorts or a head to toe Burka.

People learn culture from childhood on and feel comfortable within those patterns of thinking and behaving. Herein lies much of the problem for many HSPs. Since culture is continually being renegotiated by its members, the individuals who are the majority, exert the greatest influence on the patterns of life. HSPs are a large minority and often fall outside the range of what is considered "normal" behavior.

In my survey, 49% of HSPs strongly agreed with the statement "HSPs are not understood and appreciated in my culture" a further 39% agreed.

For instance, if a social group is being noisy and boisterous, it is likely many HSPs would, after a time, feel a need to withdraw, due to feeling frazzled by the absorption of other's energies. The rest of the group may feel no such need and continue for some time, depending on the event. The HSP may be labeled as antisocial, too quiet, or neurotic. In a work context, these impressions become powerful stigmatizing tools with which coworkers and superiors affirm group bonds and hierarchies. The HSP, by withdrawing sooner than others, may be seen as lower in status and as not fitting in. In a teamwork-obsessed workplace, this can be disastrous.

Culture, because it is so arbitrary, is constantly being reevaluated by its members with new beliefs and patterns instituted as the generations come and go. This is a positive for HSPs because in a society where greater diversity is being encouraged, and tolerance of differing traits, in general, is slowly becoming mainstream HSPs may find it easier to assert their needs and not feel like they have to fit in as much. There are other complexities that form our social perspective. One of the most significant of which is social class.

Social Class

One of the most significant influencing factors on our behaviors, beliefs, and worldview is the social class we hail from. Social class situates us within society at a particular level based partially on our incomes, but also our belief systems. HSPs are not predominantly from one social class but are more deeply affected by the negative ramifications of the lower class and poverty. This does not mean, however, that an HSP from a lower socioeconomic class has no potential for upward mobility. It is true, though, that if HSPs are in a situation where more social ills are present, they will be more deeply affected over time. It is also true that, to come from a lower class means that certain beliefs will not serve the HSP well, and may contribute to poor self-esteem, a diminished belief in one's ability to succeed, and lesser means and connections to build from.

Social class also seems to play an important role in the acceptance of SPS, especially during childhood. The lower social classes tend to not emphasize creativity, sensitivity, or originality, instead favoring conformity, obedience, and instrumental traits necessary for economic survival. The emphasis is on reproducing the existing social class structure, with parents assuming their children will likely work in jobs like theirs, rather than on developing individuals to their maximum potential. For HSPs, from higher socioeconomic classes, there may be more of an acceptance and appreciation for creative, sensitive individuals, based on the perception that the types of careers their children will work in will require more creativity and offer more autonomy for this type of work. Children from middle-class families are also likely to be afforded opportunities for greater development of creative capacities, through camps and workshops that enhance and strengthen creative skills and abilities. HSPs from supportive, nurturing backgrounds of this type, may be more likely to be accepted for exhibiting sensitivity.

In my survey, 48% of HSPs strongly agreed with the statement "I feel somehow different than others in my society" a further 45% agreed.

A strong majority of HSPs report feeling "different" than others in their society. In fact, we are different because we are more complex individuals! That sense of differentness is profound for many HSPs and is partly due to lack of awareness of the trait. Several participants expressed views that seem to substantiate this feeling of differentness. For instance, Astrid from Sweden and Chouko from Japan stated respectively:

"I am not the only highly sensitive person here in Denmark so, but I think I have not always liked that I am highly sensitive person because it does not fit into our society. It does not fit in,

and I think a lot of people think the same way as I do. I think that they do not fit in and even though they can feel I need to rest now, they don't listen to them self, because they don't know much about it." (Astrid)

"People think that highly sensitive people are neurotic, not highly sensitive or introvert. I see many highly sensitive extraverts here because they speak up. Oh, it is too bright. It is too loud. Those people probably have a more difficult time here. It is because people do not like them here. Being introvert is very accepted here. We call people shy. Shy is not a bad thing or negative here. It is just shy. Shy means we should not force her to do things or force her to speak. She is just shy. It does not mean negative to me or to other people. Over stimulating things that is a problem." (Chouko)

Awareness of HSPs in the population likely varies a great deal, based on social class, with those for whom survival is predominantly being less able or interested in differences in innate temperaments. For those whom everyday survival is less of an issue, there is likely a greater awareness and appreciation of personality differences. This stratification is somewhat problematic for HSPs, but not unduly so because awareness of HSPs, in general, is low, but on the rise. However, awareness does not necessarily lead to acceptance or appreciation. For those from the lower classes, even a heightened societal awareness may take a backseat to practical considerations, but the picture is, as usual, complex.

Regardless of the socioeconomic background you came from, you possess certain very admirable qualities of mind as a highly sensitive person. Among these is a deep complexity of mind that enables you to think ahead and plan alternatives, an innate creative ability that includes divergent thinking and innovative problem solving, deep empathy which allows you to enter the experience of another person, and the ability to notice subtle details others would miss. In almost every capacity imaginable, these are tremendous plusses in a working environment. Your socioeconomic class situates you in a place but does not necessarily consign you to it forever. Social class is negotiable as one grows and evolves, leaving behind beliefs, behaviors, and worldviews. Though we loosely divide these into categories, labeled as a particular social class, who and what you come to embody ultimately is, largely, up to you.

There are some limitations of upward mobility that should be considered. Research has shown that, for those from the lower and underclasses, a post-secondary education will not benefit them as much as it would for those from the middle or upper classes. This is due to the advantage others already have in place, regarding connections and influence enabling them to access the hidden job market. Most jobs never make it to an advertisement and are instead filled from within through connections. This represents quite a difficulty for the HSP who is not as social, not as connected, and who does not enjoy the benefits of external help. I come from such a background. In my evaluation, it is still worthwhile to expand one's horizons as much as possible with no regard for how well others are doing or for how much further one might be along the career path with the right help. The reality is, for many of us, the progress we can make in one lifetime is enough to substantially differentiate us from backgrounds and social class links we do not wish to be associated with.

Gender

To date we have looked at culture and social class. We have learned that both are somewhat permeable and impermanent as each generation negotiates its own belief systems while casting off some outdated beliefs. Gender is another aspect of the sociological picture we are developing that has a major impact on how HSPs experience life and work.

I knew that being a highly sensitive male would be much more problematic than for females before I conducted any research. Males in western societies, especially America, are constrained by narrow views regarding masculinity, with certain aspects like aggression and competitiveness, prized over an emotional life or creativity. In other words, in American society, and many other western societies, males are expected to exhibit the instrumental traits associated with traditional masculinity that typically eschew the more feminine we associate as expressive, like cooperation, nurturing, and emotionality. From the initial study, here are a few quotes that bring to bear this imbalance many highly sensitive males felt and perceived:

It became more obvious through experience that sensitivity was something that I needed to keep to myself. It was basically a punishable offense, not in school, but with my dad. He was not respectful of that trait in me at all... I grew up with a father who was very, very hostile to who I was...It was particularly difficult for me, because being sensitive it seemed like everything I did was too slow, it was wrong, you know just not acceptable, not what he wanted, and I had problems in school and gym classes and so forth. I seem to be kind of clumsy. I did not really pick things up in terms of physical skills, because that is what the other boys did. I would get punished for that. Sometimes I just got shamed and struck in front of the other kids, so that made me feel stupid, like I was just incapable of doing things like that. As I got into high school, I really wanted to be part of the male peer group and so I went ahead and did sports anyway. I went out and raved and ranted and all that stuff, but it did not come easily to me, so I could be part of a peer group. I also did a bunch of stuff that I really did not want to do, because I did not want to be seen as a pussy or whatever the boys put on each other. I think that in some ways I made some necessary adjustments so that I would not feel ostracized, but it was not necessarily because I felt comfortable doing those things. (Kirk)

In my survey, 20% of male HSPs disagreed with the statement "My father accepted me as a sensitive boy," 6% agreed.

I tried to play in sports. I played football, but I was not, I mean, I did not like playing and I did not drive as hard as I could have and I didn't hit as hard as I could have. Almost like participating in life, but not quite...Now looking in retrospect at my life, I see that I was way over stimulated all the time. Especially being around a father who I could not do anything right. He would easily spit down on me to cuss me out or take a swing at me. I got highly sensitive to my environment. It did not take much to set me off. I had a hot temper for a lot of years. I would just explode in an instant. (Joshua)

I wasn't able to make decisions quick enough, so she would scream and yell as my father would...I remember as a kid, you know, crying and my dad coming in and saying shut up and I stopped crying. He walked out and my mom said go ahead and cry...I played football for five years, which that was a challenge being who I was, because I am a big guy, I am six foot three...I remember the coach telling me to go to the game and just spit on the guy in front of me, so spit on him, and tell him that you slept with his sister. I was like, I had never had sex before, I was kind of very shy in a really big kid's body and I came out of the game and he said, "Did you do it?" I said "No," and I could not lie, you know. He said, "you are a nice guy Kurt and that is not good." He just walked away very disappointed with me, right... I remember that story because that is the general attitude, you know, kind of systemic around the limitations of what men can be...that is the challenge with my father, with his expectations of what men should be and how he were raised. (Kurt)

In my initial study, two participants were military veterans, three played competitive sports in high school or college, four were high sensation-seeking HSPs, and one identified as gay. Additionally, eight were from unsupportive childhoods with their deviations from a full expression of hegemonic masculinity serving as a primary catalyst for emotional and physical abuse from others, particularly fathers. The participant who identified as gay, though he experienced an overall supportive childhood, reported shaming and abuse for his effeminate expression of his gender.

The worldview where males are expected to exhibit a narrow interpretation of what society deems to be acceptable is deleterious to many HSPs because it inherently limits who we are "supposed" to be. To intentionally suppress parts of ourselves is to push those aspects into what Carl Jung called the Shadow. These elements do not simply disappear. They crop up from time to time often reasserting their existence and causing much inner turmoil and conflict for the individual and for society.

In my survey, 22% of male HSPs agreed with the statement "I learned to hide my sensitivities as a male," 8% disagreed.

For many people, it is not until mid-life that they begin to feel a tug towards integration of their entire beings. For HSPs, the same may hold true, but what I sensed from the male HSPs, that I interviewed was an expression of masculinity that would not wait to integrate itself.

The male HSPs in my study, described a psychological and emotional androgyny that was inclusive of instrumental and expressive traits, in relatively equal proportions. In real terms, this means the men are not afraid to be fully human, to have the courage to embody more than mere cultural conditioning, and to use this embodiment for altruistic purposes. As Kurt, Bruce, and Kirk explained,

I really believe that we embody feminine and masculine energies and I think systemically that the feminine has been crushed in an attempt to assassinate that within myself and outside of myself. I think that if we can accept those parts of ourselves and not just accept them but nurture them. I think when we do that, it can help with a lot of things. I think a lot of folks are just trapped in those kinds of concepts of what a man should be and what a woman should be. (Kurt)

I tend to look at stuff on the small scale and each individual. For example, for me, my relationships with the kids in the after school program was great because in some way my goal was to redefine masculinity with the males there...they had a lot of anger there and to just be sensitive enough to say, ok, well how can I just listen to them and be open to that and say, yeah, your feelings are valid or you have the right to be angry where you are at and to give them a platform to talk about that. I think if I would want to redefine masculinity that would be it, just allow males to be able to express their feelings in a way that is healing. (Bruce)

As I have gotten farther along in life. I have begun to own more of who I am because I need to be happy. I do not seem to have the energy for it anymore. I must do it all day at work, and I do

not want to have to do it the rest of the time. In some ways, I have fewer friends now than I did when I was younger, because I have a better sense of who I am. I just realized that I do not have unlimited time. That just changed my whole perspective of what mattered to me or what was important. I went through a year or two, after that, where I just did not even know if I wanted to be here anymore, because it was so miserable in my job. I guess what I am trying to get to, is I sort of reasoned down my life in terms of its priority on the basis of at the moment of my death how am I going to see this? Am I going to feel like I was everything I could be, as authentic as I can be to the best of my ability or am I going to feel like I was just kind of making sacrifices to fit in with other people and do what they want? That just clarified everything for me. (Kirk)

In my survey, 88% of male HSPs agreed with the statement "I am not a traditional male."

It's clear to me, and I hope the reader, that if there is one area of HSP research that needs much more work, it is in reconciling male HSPs in a way that is healing and empowering. If we zoom back out and look at gender from a career standpoint, it does not seem to matter whether the individual is male or female, as long as they are able to fulfill the needs of the position. In that sense, gender lines should be permeable with each person fully able and accepted for their integration of instrumental (typically thought of as masculine) and expressive (typically thought of as feminine). This sentiment, likely, would work better in some regions than in others, where traditional ideas still retain a grip on the beliefs of many people.

We did not speak in any meaningful sense about female gender roles. Most the participants in my initial study expressed that they felt being an HSP, and being a female, was far more acceptable than for males. Emotionality has long been equated with being female, thus it is more acceptable overall for females to exhibit behaviors that would be congruous with societal expectations.

The intricate web of complexity revealed

Culture, social class, and gender are only a few of the factors affecting our positioning in society. Group affiliations play a huge role, as well, and are especially applicable to our discussion of the workplace, where we spend so much time. Each group has its own spoken and unspoken rules, with rewards and sanctions, as they apply to behavior. Acceptance by our peer groups motivates many of us to conform. We all desire a sense of belonging and it is this frustrated need that often causes HSPs so much grief. HSPs are often the most conscientious members of any group, yet, very often, feel like outsiders or out of place. HSPs, however, can be full group members and establish identities that are very secure. Our perceptions of acceptance many times are off, and we think or feel that others do not like us, do not think we are worthwhile, or feel otherwise ostracized. In some cases, any of these items may be true, but my instinct is that, at least, some of the time, we HSPs allow our thoughts to run away with themselves. *We are not so very different in the end. Human beings all have similar needs for belonging, acceptance, love, and support from our fellow beings.*

In the big picture, that we have woven in this chapter, we see that we are born into a particular situation that largely determines our perceptions, beliefs, and values, but that these are negotiable and not necessarily limiting factors. We have looked at gender and determined it is entirely arbitrary and that many male HSPs are happily living beyond the bounds of narrow gender roles. Lastly, we have determined that our position in society is complex, dynamic, and changeable. This chapter has been more theoretical than practical but to completely understand the context within which HSPs live and work it was necessary to touch on the most important factors.

Advice for HSPs

Q: At my work, I always feel like there is a power struggle going on as people try to sabotage others. I do not know what to make of it other than it is an insane way to live.

A: Sociology provides us with tools to clarify power struggles. One is a theory called conflict theory, by Karl Marx. Marx's theory originated as a means of explaining the power struggles that he witnessed, at the beginning of the Industrial Revolution, but have since been adapted to help us better understand imbalances in power relationships in many aspects of life. In a work context, most company cultures tend to be hierarchical, with stratified levels of authority and prestige. When the imbalances between those who have very little to lose and those who seem to have more struggles to usurp their perceived power are common, perhaps even natural for people. This tendency is not aided by the for-profit basis many western societies are founded on where exploitation and manipulation aided by complicit politicians prevail. When people have nothing to lose, they resort to extreme measures to obtain resources, or they give up. HSPs, in some cases, may feel this giving up reaction as a defense mechanism, and it is difficult to work in such an environment.

Q: In my culture HSPs are not well known or understood. Should I tell others that I feel I am an HSP?

A: There is no reason to tell anyone what your personality traits are. Your abilities and talents will likely speak for themselves and, if they don't, revealing something that you probably feel very deeply about to others who are not receptive to, or aware of, what you're saying will be non-productive. Share when you feel it is appropriate, to people you feel are receptive, but it is not necessary to feel any obligation to reveal that you are a highly sensitive person.

Q: I grew up in a lower-class working family where I felt very different from everyone else. How do I become what and who I feel I am meant to be?

A: Social class, as we have examined, is a set of stratified beliefs, behaviors, and worldviews. The challenge for the HSP who wishes to "break out" of a confining social class is to adopt new beliefs, behaviors, and worldviews. This is not an easy thing to do but is made easier if you can objectively examine your beliefs over time and discard those that do not work for you. I do not advocate adopting any social classes' beliefs, behaviors, or worldviews wholesale. Instead, decide for yourself what you will believe, how you will act, and how you will see the world. We are all unique individuals, and should make up our own minds, even with pressures to conform. In time, you will feel comfortable with who you are becoming and feel confident in your choices.

Q: I have always felt conflicted about gender like I am more equally parts masculine and feminine. This makes me feel like something is wrong with me because I am not "one of the guys." How do I reconcile these feelings?

A: Gender is arbitrary and formulated by each culture. What is entirely normal in one is entirely abnormal in another. My advice is be who you are and do it with confidence. It is perfectly okay to embody a masculinity that is inclusive of nurturing, cooperation, and emotional expression. In fact, the world needs individuals who are more psychologically and emotionally androgynous. Group pressures to conform are powerful and designed to reinforce existing notions of gender, but they only matter if you allow it to. Find and associate with people who are more like you, where you will find acceptance. Life is too short to not enjoy the sense of connection between people when conditions are right.

Q: Has race played a significant factor in the lives of HSPs?

A: For some, yes, but, in my survey, over 75% of HSPs disagreed that their experience of race has been more important in their lives than their experience of high sensitivity. Undoubtedly, one would need to study specific groups if the intent were to establish a truer picture of the role race plays in the lives of any one group because the experience of race is so closely tied to culture and social class.

Part III

Part three of this book comprises two large chapters. The first, specifically discusses careers for HSPs, including virtual home workers, self-employment, and trade/vocational work. Each section in chapter eight will, no doubt, appeal to certain HSPs more than others, because some HSPs are very interested in working from home or in being self-employed. In each case, there are several complexities that I have attempted to unravel for you to make your task easier when it comes to deciding exactly what to do.

In chapter nine, you will find several narratives from actual HSPs, who participated in my studies. These stories from HSPs, cover a wide range of topics and speak to the vast range of careers we HSPs choose and the challenges we encounter,

as we work to reconcile our inner lives with the external world. The stories, at times, touched me very deeply as they were related to me in interviews. I was left with an abiding admiration and respect for the sense of resilience and fortitude many HSPs display when faced with what is often a harsh, unforgiving world. The image problem HSPs experience from carrying the label "highly sensitive," with its implicit, societally loaded connotations of personal weakness or fragility was thoroughly debunked as I witnessed the courage and strength these HSPs communicated to me through their absolutely honest narratives. The sheer force of emotion, compassion, and intellect spoke to what I felt was a passionate fire burning brightly in the hearts of these beautiful individuals.

Chapter 8

Careers for HSPs

What career should an HSP choose? That is a tremendously complex question when we consider that there are over one billion HSPs on the planet from differing cultures, personality types, familial backgrounds, and each with a set of lived experiences and personal expectations. Many are gifted, many are not. Most HSPs are innately predisposed toward creativity, but not necessarily in the common vision of producing an end product, rather in being aware of subtleties, possessing a curiosity and an exploratory nature. A career that will work for one person will not work for another person.

In this chapter, I will present and discuss the results of a large survey conducted to understand better the types of careers of the 965 survey takers who chose to answer this question. In any survey, the results are always reflective of the people who took the survey. In this case, the results will reflect a predominantly female population because female HSPs historically volunteer more readily for studies than do males. This, perhaps, denotes a limitation of the results, but it is a sizable survey and should be gleaned for every bit of information possible. This chapter will also cover some new and old types of work with an emphasis on their applicability to HSPs.

Top career fields for HSPs (as indicated in the survey)

1. Education and training – 18.86%

2. Arts and Communications – 13.37%

3. Human services - 10.57%

4. Health Sciences – 10.24%

5. Business management and administration – 8.60%

6. Information technology – 7.98%

7. Marketing, sales, and service – 6.01%

8. Science, technology, and engineering – 6.01%

9. Government and public administration – 4.46%

10. Law, public safety, and security - 3.21%

11. Finance – 2.80%

12. Agriculture, food, and natural resources – 2.59%

13. Hospitality and tourism – 1.87%

14. Architecture and construction - 1.35%

15. Manufacturing - 1.04%

16. Transportation and distribution - 1.04%

I included a space in the survey question for HSPs to fill in the blank with personal notes and 352 survey takers provided specific details about their careers. I present most of the 352 with duplicate positions omitted. This is truly a fascinating panorama of the HSP kaleidoscope of careers!

Administration in Music - retired self-employed horticulture business owner - Computer Games Industry - Alternative Healing – Philanthropy - Market Research - specialty store owner - House/pet sitter – physician - Interactivity, Design and

Storytelling - Unfocused & Unemployed – Horticulture - Theatrical costume design and construction - Registered Nurse in ICU and ER - Executive Search reference Specialist - Engineering design - homemaker/part-time French teacher - Non-Profit, community outreach - Engineer and stay-at-home mom - retired civil/environmental engineer - Circus Arts/Performance – Pastor – Counseling - social change - Social Science Research - Coaching & Consulting - Landscape/Gardening - Music Education - Disabled or retired - Writer and Editor –

Psychotherapist and Bodyworker - Nursing and professor at university – Teacher - Health Science + IT - Astrology teacher & Counselor/Volunteer - In Between! Working on pottery. Learning energy healing to start my own practice! - Musician, Special Needs Music Teacher and Composer - Massage Therapist – Cosmetology – Psychotherapy – military – Linguistics - 20 yrs. law enforcement, now an artist as of 2007!! - Real estate - Currently in graduate program in mental health counseling - Certified Clinical Hypnotherapist - Career and vocational advising (rehabilitation) - Professional Ballet Dancer and Instructor - working on finishing a first novel - Environmental Conservation - Soldier and physician – arts, I teach singing and performance, but also working with a network marketing company offering legal plans - Event planner - transitioning from public elem. teacher in CA, to art educator in an art museum, to working on opening a private, democratically-run school like Sudbury Valley School - Retired art teacher--now a private piano teacher - I have two jobs. I am an adjunct university instructor, and a government health policy analyst - Geriatric nursing and rehab - Teacher, massage therapist, health coach, and professional musician - User-centered digital service design.

Stay at home mom/homeschool teacher – Entrepreneur - long-term Medicaid Consultant [self-employed] - Independent Artist - Program evaluation - not for profit. International development – therapist, children, and youth, transformation coach/trainer adults - Administration in Higher Education - 2 jobs: 1. Counsellor (fulfilling), 2. Admin (less so) - Metaphysical Studies - Organizational Coach and Writer - Academia, a combination of arts, science, education – shaman - Graphic Design - Freelance translator.

Psychology - Self-Employed Bookkeeper - ngo children's helpline - Freelance Writer/Editor for a range of industry sectors - I'm both a nutritionist and a journalist who covers food and nutrition - executive coach and entrepreneur - Health Professional (Occupational Therapist/Psychotherapist) - Dog Handler, Kennel Worker – Spa - Real Estate Appraiser- Self-Employed - Industrial Maintenance Mechanic - Retired university research administration - music / classical singer - Creative & Multi-disciplinary Design - Retired, US Air Force Officer - Helicopter pilot - teach yoga and meditation - Geophysical modelling – self-employed - speech therapist - Health Care, Religion and Ethics - Non-profits, museums- Art Jeweler // Columnist // working on a novel - Food Service Manager.

Freelance science writer - Pet/animal services - Nursing Home Housekeeping - Volunteer at Nature Center & Bird Sanctuary - I'm a ghostwriter for an integrative/holistic veterinarian - Yoga instructor, life coach - Inventor and Philosophy/Spiritual Writer - Children emotional health - No job for the last 4 years - Medical Receptionist - Writer, freelance editor, independent print-on-demand book publisher - Psychology/Spirituality - Musician, Music teacher, Music therapist (licensed), Equine-assisted therapies - Translation in human rights - antique restoration - Unable to work due to high anxiety - clinical psychotherapist and researcher in psychology - Self-employed, writer and animal rights activist - retired elementary school counselor - Educational interpreting - My career is in the Natural Environment. My current employer is the Faculty of Science and Technology at a post-secondary institution - Assistant Librarian for an Academic Learning Institution such as a University – Biotechnology.

Analysis – what does this all mean?

I grouped these notes into categories to learn if they would fit into the same categories previously identified by percentages, and, interestingly, there were a few notable exceptions. First, self-employed did not have a response available on the survey, and I would be remiss if I did not give voice to that category. Though the education and creative fields dominated by fair margins, self-employment represent a solid third place. I grouped the responses like counseling, psychology, and coaching into a healing category along with medical professionals, or what was represented by human services and health sciences in the survey, and arrived at a cumulative total eclipsing both education and the creative fields. What does this mean? I offer a few main points for your consideration:

• Though the education and creative fields may be tremendously rewarding the healing or helping professions offer a direct one-on-one sense of meaningfulness, whereby, an individual may see tangible, immediate results in another person's physical or emotional health or well-being.

• HSPs involved in education are dispersed quite broadly from the humanities to STEM fields.

• HSPs in the creative fields, tend toward writing with many freelancers. Music and music education also appear to be prominent. It is likely that other HSPs are in many other areas of creativity such as painting, sculpting, pottery, printmaking, dance, and the theater.

• HSPs, in self-employment, appear to do well in services related to pets, animals, plants, landscaping, and other areas utilizing careful planning, connection with nature, and empowering others.

• HSPs, in the healing fields, appear to prefer helping others with their emotional lives, somatic concerns, and spiritual/contemplative practices.

• In the non-profit sector, HSPs seem to concern themselves with social action, animal welfare, strengthening communities locally and internationally, and environmental protection and conservation.

The remaining responses may seem atypical for HSPs, but HSPs may do quite well in STEM (science, technology, engineering, and mathematics) fields given the right conditions. HSPs may also do quite well in certain military specialties, depending on the individual, and government careers. It is also likely that some of the lesser categories like transportation and distribution would include positions that would work well for some HSPs like drivers, material handlers, or supervisors responsible for planning. Many positions of this nature offer autonomy and stability as well as the engagement of capacities.

If you will recall our discussion of Csikszentmihalyi's conceptualization of the flow state, it is when an individual is matched regarding abilities to task and has a sense of potential control. The task itself is irrelevant. It does not matter whether one is working as a carpenter or a programmer; it is a matter of the individual's ability being matched to the task in ways that promote growth. The flow experience itself needs to become autotelic, which if you recall, means it is worth doing for its own sake. Now, let us look at a few specific fields that hold, what I feel, is promise for HSPs.

Virtual work

With the changes that have taken place in the workplace in the past few decades, the possibility of working from home at a job that pays well has become more real than ever before, for some. I preface that promise with the word 'some,' because the best virtual work positions require experience, education, and an affiliation with companies or organizations who have realized the benefit to them, concerning economics and efficiency.

Examples of virtual work

What do we mean by virtual work? Virtual work can also be thought of as remote work or working from home. You might be as surprised, as I was, to learn that 34 million workers already work from home! It is estimated by a 2009 Forrester report that, by 2016, 43% of the US workforce will be working from home. That is 63 million workers, and that is just in the US. The trend is likely global and will only increase as workers express their preferences to employers and employers seek to recruit and retain top talent. Sounds great right? You get to work from home on your schedule with none of the distractions of an office environment, but is it really all it seems to be cracked up to be? Not exactly, and we should be very careful here in delineating which workers do best in a work from home arrangement.

Advantages of virtual work

The number one advantage to HSPs would have to be autonomy. By autonomy, we mean the ability of an individual to freely carry out assigned duties and tasks with minimal supervision of interference. HSPs absolutely prize this quality! There are many benefits to autonomous work arrangements for HSPs. First, the pressure of feeling as if one is being watched is lessened. Many HSPs strongly dislike feeling as if eyes are always on them .

The second advantage, and the biggest contributor to an increase in productivity in virtual work, is a quieter work environment free of distractions, office chatter, and noises. HSPs are not the only ones bothered by distracting working conditions, but we are more intensely affected by noisy, distracting conditions than others and benefit more from quiet conditions that support intense focus and involvement in the task. Quieter conditions also promote better overall health with lower stress, less anxiety, and greater job satisfaction.

The third advantage is a flexible work schedule where one can more adequately meet the needs of family life, care for an elderly parent, or accommodate other unique conditions that typify the modern world. When workers are more able to meet their overall needs in a way that promotes a feeling of reasonable control, the result is greater productivity and job satisfaction. However, not all people end up liking or staying in virtual work positions. Let us look at a few of the very real disadvantages and why we might reconsider virtual work or work from home arrangements.

Opportunities for HSPs to shine in virtual work

According to Sean Graber in the Harvard Business Review, successful remote work needs to be based on three core principles: communication, coordination, and culture.

Communication – clearly communicating complex ideas relies on more than a simple email. We often underestimate the amount of social information we take in during a face to face conversation, including body language, inflections, and gestures. In a virtual world, many of these cues are missing unless video conferences or short video messages are utilized along with frequent communications that allow for asking pertinent questions. Virtual workers are often in different time zones in varying parts of the world.

HSPs may be at an advantage in composing emails or short videos, where one is able to rehearse or edit what is said before sending the message because we prefer to carefully think through a problem or statement before we make it. HSPs also spend more time gathering visual information in a given scene. This may make us more suitable in an ironic way for virtual work than others who would not spend as long interpreting the visual cues in a recorded video message or teleconference. In this sense, we can turn a disadvantage for non-HSPs into an advantage for HSPs.

Coordination – ensuring that a team of virtual workers is all on the same page can be like herding cats! Concurrent with the above-mentioned communication, the need to coordinate individual efforts to reach goals, requires that everyone knows what others are doing and how it all fits into the larger goal. Creating formal processes that make all information available to all workers and the modeling of appropriate process behaviors by managers is imperative. HSPs may be at an advantage here, as well, because we are natural planners and organizers with a deep need for things done well. If HSPs are one thing, it is conscientious, and we will sweat out the details with a big picture focus. That is who we are and what we do naturally.

Highly sensitive people prefer to do everything well regarding planning and execution, but that same conscientiousness does not necessarily carry over to all workers and HSPs may find themselves saddled with team members whose standards may be lower. This can be a potential stumbling point for HSPs because our tolerance for poor work is low and we will react to those who do shoddy or substandard work. Though this may be upsetting for the HSP, this built-in quality assurance may be a tremendous plus for the work group and organization.

Culture – what do we mean by culture? Culture is composed of material and non-material considerations. Material culture includes everything in the physical world we are familiar with. The non-material culture includes intangibles such as group values, morals, and ethics. The need to belong, and feel as if we are bonded to others, is an extremely strong instinct in human beings, and HSPs are no exception. Building an effective virtual culture that mirrors the organization's goals and values is essential to inculcate a sense of belonging in all virtual workers.

Graber argues that there are two types of trust that are essential to fostering engagement and sustaining performance for virtual workers. The first, is cognitive trust, based on competence and reliability. HSPs would likely establish themselves on this aspect quickly due to our conscientiousness. The second, is affective trust, based on feeling. For HSPs, this may be relatively easy, as we utilize our strong empathy to "feel a person" out or difficult, as in a situation where HSPs are paired with others who are hard to read or who deliberately change their behaviors. In both cases, HSPs would be at an advantage, due to our high empathy which would enable us to intuitively know whether we should trust the others in a work group.

Limitations of virtual work

Working from home may seem ideal for many HSPs, but at closer inspection, there are some downsides worth considering that may prove pivotal in deciding whether working from home is right for you. The first is loneliness. Loneliness may be the furthest thing from your mind as you contemplate leaving that noisy, distracting office environment, but it is the primary reason virtual workers return to the office, according to study by Bloom and Roberts.5 Loneliness for HSPs may be mitigated by the increase in autonomy, flexible work schedule and freedom from overstimulation or irritating daily conditions, but let's recall again that HSPs process all stimulation more deeply than do others. Loneliness may trigger depression, lethargy, and anxiety regarding deadlines and bring into question the issue of sustainably working from home.

A full half of the home workers in Bloom and Robert's study decided to return to the office, after the study ended, and three-quarters of those who stayed in the office, as a control group, decided to remain in the office environment. The individuals who seemed to prefer homework were typically high performers, who benefit from the quieter home environment. The distraction-free home environment is obviously very attractive to the high performer, and I would include many HSPs among these. The individuals who decide the office environment is preferable are likely more extraverted and need social interaction, more than would the 70% of more introverted HSPs. It's worth noting, as well, that the study took place in Ctrips' Shanghai headquarters call center, which was likely staffed by Asians from a more communally oriented culture. For Westerners, from a more individualized cultural background, the need to excel on an individual level may be stronger.

A second limitation of working from home may be the home environment itself. Not everyone lives in the best home or has spaces that one would wish to be in for such long periods of time. For some people, the extra time at home may be more than they care for. Family members may assume that, because you are always home, you are not actually doing anything and, so, feel free to distract you with requests or unwanted visits. Establishing and maintaining firm boundaries between work time and off time would be even more critical in that case, and *many HSPs already have significant issues with setting boundaries.* Some HSPs may prefer the relative sanity of a structured, dedicated office environment over their home environment. Assuming one can set up a disciplined structure to function within is far easier said than done. As the study indicated, the high performers benefited the most from working from home with the implicit assumption they were also able to provide their own disciplined structure to work from. Others may be happier in the office environment, even given its inherent distractions.

Many office environments are changing with more emphasis on the needs of workers who are demanding greater autonomy, more flexible working spaces, flexible work assignments that allow the workers to decide what they work on, and more diffusion of central authority to work teams. This counterbalancing mechanism to virtual work may make the office environment, in many cases, as suitable as a home environment for many. However, it is likely there are some HSPs who would always prefer to work from home and for those individuals virtual work and the professions and careers that most employ them should be at the top of their list.

Virtual work, while a distinct possibility for some HSPs, may be only part of a larger picture of autonomous actions that generate income. Another such endeavor is self-employment, which is a mere sleight of hand from working from home in some ways, but vastly different and more complex in others.

Self-Employment

Self-employment may seem like the greatest gig ever, considering that you are able to largely call your own shots, determine your income, and generally experience a greater degree of freedom and autonomy than is possible in traditional employment. As with all human endeavors, the truth is more complex, and there are some important upsides and downsides we should consider when contemplating the suitability of self-employment for HSPs. To do that, let us look at some of the most common assumptions regarding the self-employed and weigh them through an HSP lens.

• Risk – many people worry about the amount of financial and personal risk involved in being self-employed and, rightly so, because it can be a complex and complicated process in the beginning. There are numerous processes and protocols that must be worked out and followed for legal, financial, and viability reasons. The good news is, the learning curve may seem steeper than it is, and, once one has started a small business, successive small businesses will be much easier. For HSPs, the uncertainty and ambiguity in initial income, may produce extensive anxiety, so much so that traditional employment may seem preferable. The risk, however, is always calculated, and HSPs are usually good at thinking through complexities and minimizing risks.

• Long hours – it is true many self-employed people work longer hours than do their counterparts, but if they have chosen a business they love the work may not seem like work. Instead, the line between work and home becomes blurred with a nearly effortless movement from one to the other in the best of cases. In the worst cases, small business offers the opportunity to shut down operations and start over at something more suitable. The hours one works are greatly variable and depend on the type of business. It is possible to build a business with a reasonable compromise between hours worked and hours desired.

• Stress – the ability to potentially control one's day to a large extent is perhaps the best reason for an HSP to become self-employed. There are, however, numerous stresses like meeting deadlines, dealing with suppliers and customers, and continually having to source new business clients. These stresses may be as great as, or greater than, employment depending on one's last position. Self-employment offers the opportunity to lower stress in several ways. For one, there is total control over one's physical environment. Self-employed people are free to arrange workspaces that work for them and rearrange without asking anyone for permission. For another, it may be possible to structure one's working hours to suit individual preferences. Flexible working hours are becoming increasingly popular in employment, but self-employment offers absolute control, with only the demands of the business dictating what needs to be accomplished and when.

• Social – in self-employment one can avoid negative stimulation by not dealing with customers or clients who decide to be obnoxious or abrasive. This freedom generally does not exist in employment. One is also free to hire employees who will be compatible with the company culture, that you have chosen to establish, and not hire those who will prove disruptive or undermine morale. For the HSP, being able to largely control the social aspects of their interactions may be a huge advantage and justify the risks and anxieties involved in self-employment. Self-employment also offers the opportunity to socialize with other business owners with like minds. Being able to bond with others, involved in a similar venture, may be rewarding beyond levels achievable by income generated in any business.

• Sole responsibility – the sheer complexity of running a business may seem overwhelming for many HSPs, because we have a need to ensure everything is done well. Our innate conscientiousness prevents us from glossing over the complications that need to be thought through. The fear of this complexity may be paralyzing, yet we know businesses exist everywhere and seem to handle the complexity well. The key knowledge points that HSPs need to bear in mind is that we must leverage other systems to cover our accounting, production, shipping, and advertising. It is not necessarily a matter of each business owner doing everything. Rather, they hire or contract with skilled others who can carry out tasks. It is simply a matter of putting the right individuals in the right positions. This is true, even for a one-person business, where bookkeeping or other administrative functions may be sourced out to other small businesses. In the end, though, you are responsible for everything that happens in your business and everything that does not happen.

Self-employment may offer many significant advantages

for HSPs. These advantages carry some degree of inherent risk and ambiguity that may or may not be tolerable or preferable for any one person. For the HSP, coming from a corporate background, where basic needs for autonomy, appropriate socialization, a sense of competence, and growth opportunities are not met, self-employment may be a very viable alternative to lingering longer than necessary in work that does not work.

As with virtual work, self-employment will not be appropriate for every person and the costs versus benefits must be carefully thought through before embarking on a new business venture. Once one has made the decision to start a business, it should be worked at very diligently and with great patience, as success may take more than the initial startup year. There are several avenues one may take to become self-employed. Some people will find it best to remain in their current job, while building up their business on the side. Others will find it best to do half and half, with employment always remaining as part of the overall picture. One obvious small business that may be built up while retaining paid employment is especially suitable for some HSPs: the fine arts and crafts.

Fine art and crafts work

Many HSPs are very talented individuals who are working in creative fields, like painting, pottery, sculpture, printmaking, fiber art, independent filmmaking, photography, and a hundred other possibilities. While I have generally defined creativity in broader terms here, I am referring to producing an end product such as pottery, painting, or film. I have known and worked with, and for, individuals who owned and operated small studios producing everything from very fine ceramic pots to high-end oil paintings. Opening your own studio, where you produce your own, original work may be the avenue you want to pursue if you are willing to learn how to operate a small business and have developed your skills and talents.

A wise potter once told me that an aspiring craftsperson or artist needs to, first, learn how to run a business, then acquire the necessary skill development. This reasoning is sound on several levels, and I advocate for HSPs heeding this advice as they contemplate owning and operating a functioning studio. Artistic development need not take place in an expensive art school. One can learn a great deal through community colleges, single classes taken at universities, and even from artists and craftspeople themselves. Often working studios hold classes to teach interested people the skills of painting, producing pottery, printmaking, photography, and a multitude of other creative expressions. The possibility may exist to do an apprenticeship, or work as a studio assistant, which is an avenue I chose, when I wanted to learn the real ins and outs of producing and selling handmade pottery. The amount of real-world knowledge that I gained in a short time was invaluable and not an experience I could have acquired in a school.

With this encouraging possibility, I want to temper it with the real-world concerns of running a business. Even a skilled craftsperson or artist is fundamentally a small businessperson and as subject to the vagaries of the economy as any corporation. In fact, this is more the case because a small business is less able to weather poor economic times and will find themselves struggling sooner than a corporation with reserves. It is for that reason, that I advocate starting an art studio while still employed. Paid employment will provide a buffer for the unexpected times and provide you with time and money to acquire the necessary equipment. In a pottery operation, for instance, the equipment needs are equal to a small manufacturing operation and requires a dedicated space. Add to that the costs of promoting and selling work on the art show circuit, and the financial requirements may be daunting. It is not surprising that many craftspeople and artists work as teachers or otherwise hold paid employment.

The potential for a skilled artist or craftsperson to own and operate a working studio, where one is able to create an atmosphere where creativity, autonomy, and cross-fertilization thrive may make the risks entirely worth it. There are many successful, full-time artists and craftspeople who would not trade their way of life for anything. For some HSPs, owning and operating an art studio may be exactly the outlet you have been searching for.

Another type of work that is closely tied to self-employment is often overlooked and suffers from an image problem, that I hope to repair, because I feel it offers promise for some HSPs who seek autonomy, often good income, and a chance to work on your own. What am I speaking about? Trade work or vocational work.

Trade work

There are many kinds of work at many differing levels of expertise, prestige, compensation, and requirements. Western society is largely a credential society where one must hold post-secondary educational attainment to play the mainstream game. However, that is not the only game available to play, nor is it necessarily the best. HSPs must consider many factors in searching for work that truly meets their needs. One area of work requires less education and may offer some HSPs just the situation that would work when more traditional career paths would not. Trade schools and vocational work are often thought of as less-skilled or for those with less potential, but I want to reframe it for you in new terms that offer a new perspective on an area of work that may be just what you are looking for.

The premise

All work is honorable. All work allows the individual to sustain personal dignity through their own efforts and keep body and mind together. In all frankness, trades have gotten a bad rap from our society. Individuals who are skilled in plumbing, electrical, roofing, carpentry of all types, repair work, skilled machine work, nursing, and health care related roles all provide critically necessary services to society. Without these skilled workers, society would not be able to function! Far short of relegating the trades to the less skilled I instead suggest that the trades may be a great place where you will find meaning in your work, where you will find opportunities (at a time when few may exist for the more educated), and where the inherent working conditions may actually suit your needs better than professional work.

In much of our society, there is a great deal of built-in obsolescence, instability, and insecurity. In the trades, many times the work is more secure and pays as well as many positions requiring post-secondary degrees! Granted, the work may be less desirable, in some senses, and not all HSPs will be well-suited in terms of innate temperament to exist within the role of roofer or auto mechanic, but, for those who can, they might find the work to be more self-guided, requires less intensive social interactions, and pays as well as work that may require far more in terms of preparation and upfront investment (student loans). Now, let us look at some of the ways that work in the trades may fulfill your needs as an HSP.

•   Autonomy – vocational occupations often allow one to work individually without a lot of supervision, especially the more skilled one becomes.

•   Ease of entry – the need for the trades is becoming increasingly critical, as skills are being lost in hand work of all kinds. This has created a demand in many skilled vocations.

•   Specialization – HSPs are often very good at intensely focusing on developing a skill or interest and would likely learn every facet of a given trade. Our ability to absorb information and thoroughly process what has been taught makes HSPs potentially excellent specialists. With specialization also comes the possibility of entering the state of flow where one is functioning at a peak level on challenging tasks.

•   Meaningfulness – need to do something meaningful with your time? The trades offer a way to intervene in the lives of people at critical times like when a patient is critically ill in a hospital, an individual in dire need of help may be assisted by your skills and know how, or your skills may be brought to bear for volunteerism. Being able to help someone in real need through your hands-on skills may be immensely rewarding in ways not even approachable through other careers.

•   Freedom – many tradespeople are self-employed or have the potential to become so once they are licensed, if need be. Self-employment provides the opportunity to grow a business that suits one's unique needs concerning hours worked, income produced, and individuals we choose to work with.

•   Security – many trades are very stable and will be around as long as there are people with needs. That security may be of great benefit to some HSPs who prefer secure, predictable work. There is relative security in income, as well, because, as opposed to other careers, the trades are not as subject to corporate whims and schemes to exploit workers. One can always be self-employed in the trades and eliminate the employer altogether. Lastly, knowing that your income is secure can be a solid foundation to building a life where you are free to thrive.

•   Stress – there may be less stress, in many cases, in the trades because individuals who specialize may enjoy greater autonomy in many cases, income security, a sense of control over one's life, and the possibility of altruistic activities that promote community feeling. All of these can lower stress levels and promote good health.

Limitations

Now that we have established an encouraging picture of the trades as a possibility that might work for HSPs, let us look at potential downsides. No career is without a downside, and the trades are no exception. Here are a few to consider:

•   Odd hours – some trades like nursing or plumbing may require one to be available on a 24-hour basis or to work shifts like evening, nights, holidays, or weekends. This may or may not be preferable or acceptable to an HSP, depending on one's unique circumstances. It also may work in favor of the HSP, as working odd hours generally means less intensive social interaction.

•   Harsh conditions – Tradespeople work on roofs, in basements, crawlspaces, under cars, in facilities full of germs and ill people. Many vocational workers also work outside in all weather conditions, which may not seem like an issue until it is very hot or very cold! Interpersonal conditions may also be harsh as one works alongside individuals from all socioeconomic backgrounds. This may be counterbalanced by the relative ease of choosing which employer to work for based on the specific makeup of the workers. There may be a noticeable difference among company cultures, which is easily definable.

•   Lack of growth potential – HSPs tend to be high in developmental potential and need opportunities for interesting, challenging work. Some trade work may be very routine and marginally interesting. One may move up in terms of knowledge or experience, but often reach a limit on what is possible in a given format. For some, this may not be a problem as they develop their interests outside of work. For others, this may be a built-in limitation.

•   Interpersonal – many business owners in the trades simply worked their way up to being self-employed and may or may not be suitable mentors or employers. Depending on the trade the interpersonal environment may not be intellectually stimulating enough, though there are always exceptions. Co-workers and supervisors may not be as educated or inherently interesting, if that is important to you. Lastly, you will likely encounter a wide variety of customers and clients ranging from kind and grateful to arrogant and manipulative. This may be harsh for some HSPs but may be offset by the relative freedom to simply not do business with negative clients.

The trades and vocational work offer good potential for those HSPs who may not be suited to pursuing a college education, followed by life in the corporate world. Becoming a skilled tradesperson affords one with the opportunity to work in a relatively secure, well-paying career where one can experience the flow state, do work that is directly meaningful in people's lives, and enjoy significant autonomy and freedom of action. The downsides exist with any career and should be considered, but as with many things they may seem less important or noticeable once you have been working in the field.

Advice for HSPs

Q: Do HSPs do best in any one type of career field?

A: Absolutely not. As you can see from the statistical results, earlier in this chapter, HSPs are dispersed across all career fields and are not limited by having the personality trait, sensory processing sensitivity. However, it is highly advisable to choose a career that works for you given your unique needs. Some HSPs are especially noise sensitive, in which case they would need to choose carefully. Other HSPs simply prefer to work in any of the many helping professions. It is a better idea to think of a career in an impermanent sense where what one is doing currently may not equate to what one is doing later in life. The reality of the 21st century, is that careers are inherently less stable in many cases. We need to be more flexible and open-minded to future possibilities given our skills, talents, and abilities. HSPs should work assiduously to develop strong contacts and be willing to mentor and help those who are still building their careers. One never knows who one may meet or the reciprocal possibilities that may form.

Q: I am interested in working from home and think my current employer might go for it, but I am concerned about whether it would work out. What should I do?

A: As noted in this chapter, homework is on the rise. Bear in mind that while many people are working from home, that does not necessarily mean they are home all week. Many of these positions are allowing homework on specific days and office work the rest. Others are transitioning to full-time home workers. Depending on your career field, you should investigate the possibilities that exist for you and try it out. If you are a naturally high-performing worker, homework may just be for you, if not, you may prefer the structure of an office environment.

Q: I would like to be self-employed, but have no idea where to begin.

A: There are a number of great and free resources around the US. The Small Business Administration operates many small business development centers typically associated with university campuses that can offer free help with every facet of a business startup including financing. Additionally, there are a ton of helpful books written on small business startups, but be careful there are a lot of books that are overly encouraging and that negate the risks involved or that provide useless information freely available elsewhere. Lastly, there are any number of entrepreneur groups on social media like Facebook that can offer support and encouragement from other small businesspeople. Some specifically cater to introverts or HSPs.

Q: Where can I get training for a good trade?

A: There are literally hundreds of community colleges across the US and some excellent trade-oriented schools with very good job placement records. Community colleges are specifically tasked with providing training for local citizens, appropriate for their area. Some trades offer apprenticeship programs, where one learns by apprenticing to a master tradesperson. The military also offers training in most trades that is directly transferable to the civilian world.

Chapter 9

Insights from HSPs

In this final chapter, I offer stories from real HSPs who express their sense of success with work. All have struggled to find a place in life where their way of being felt supported, sustainable, and correct for their unique temperament.

There are a few commonalities that I think are worth making explicit. First, many HSPs can move beyond considerations of overstimulation as a limiting factor and simply be in their lives, while very naturally shifting to accommodate their needs. Yes, they may feel overstimulated, but they are not paralyzed by it. Instead, they have integrated the propensity and the coping strategies into a harmonious flow that enables them to make full use of their talents and abilities. I would call these HSPs empowered individuals. Next, many HSPs fluently embody an integral emotionality with relatively equal parts masculine and feminine. In other terms, they are equally instrumental and expressive occupying both at once, without any conflict.

Lastly, HSPs are estimated to comprise 15-20% of the total population. With approximately 7 billion people on the planet, that is well over 1 billion individuals who are HSPs. For every success story, I can tell you another of struggle and heartbreak, frustration, and anguish at having such a difficult time finding work that is right for them. The success stories in this chapter are not to minimize those struggles. To the contrary, they are to light the way and provide encouragement for those who are still in the struggle.

The pressures to conform from every level of society are powerful forces. The built-in debtor status we inherit as adults tends to reign in our ability to venture out into new career territory for fear of instability. It seems to be a fact that the era of career instability is here, and it is a way of life in modern society. Technology has traditionally always outpaced ethics. Thus, we have efficiencies that have effectively reduced the need for masses of human labor (especially unskilled) and created an era of unstable work. As these notions of traditional roles crumble, we should see ourselves as free to reinvent the entire notion of work and career. It is happening all around us, and we HSPs should be the first to take advantage of the opportunities for flexibility and invent new ways of being that work for us. I offer my analysis and comments after each story.

Faith's biggest professional triumph

I had a client, he has passed away now, who had profound mental retardation. He had severe contractures of his limbs. A contracture, if you are not familiar with it, is where the muscles and ligaments have pulled so tightly that the limb is fixed. It is almost like it is so spasmed that it will not move out of that position. This individual, William, had the IQ of a two-year-old at best. He was essentially nonverbal. He was about fifty. He was in a wheelchair most of the time. He could not move himself in that wheelchair. He could get up a little bit. His feet were really swollen. He could do a little bit of getting up from his wheelchair over to a couch, and he had some other behavior difficulties.

One of the things he would do was to cry out a lot; probably we guessed in frustration. He would bite his hand. He had severe calluses on his hand from biting on it so bad. Well, one of the things we decided as a team was that it might help William and perhaps make him feel less frustrated if he could learn to propel himself in his wheelchair. The group home was a large ranch style home. It was like six bedrooms on one side and a huge living room and then a long kitchen. If you put like two ranch-style homes together and had all that length that is what it would be like.

We decided that would be a good idea and if we could get William and teach him to self-propel. He only had one hand he could really, well, he had two if he did not bite on one. His fists were kind of clutched. If we could get him to self-propel fifteen feet in a year, that would be doing really good. Well, my part was to write up the steps of the teaching module to get William to do this. I would also work with the person who worked with him, so I enjoyed doing it. That was one of my favorite things to do. I looked at it, looked at his trainer, worked with it, and figured out what to do. We, then, would go back sometimes and revise the steps as we saw what he was able to do and what he was not.

Well, it just so happened that one day, William got stuck and propelled himself a little bit, and he got stuck in the corner by the water fountain, by my office. I happened to hear him, and he was moaning, and I came out and said, "William, what is the matter?" I said, "Ok, William let us back out. I am going to show you." I did hand-over-hand with him, and I showed him how to back out, this was not in his plan at all to back out of that corner. At first, he did not get it, and I showed him again (hand-over-hand) and then he started, now mind you this is an individual with the age of a two-year-old okay? I...showed him, with his hand under mine, to back it up and then I asked him to do it. He tried. This took a few minutes, and finally, he got the hang of it, and I said, "Good, do it again," and he got it. I then said, "do it with the other hand, go forward," and showed him that way and he backed it out of that corner. I said, "Go forward," and I showed him that way, and all of the training I had been doing for two months snapped together, and he went from one side of the house to another. He never got stuck in the corner again. It was wonderful. William just let out the biggest laugh you had ever heard. I just about cried. I was like, "Oh my god, William!" All the trainers came out, and I said, "Look what William did!" and William was just laughing out loud. I said, "Oh William, that is wonderful!" I said, "Look at you! You did it!" I said, "You can go anywhere now."

The hand biting after that went way down. He was able to wheel himself all over the house. He did not go fifteen feet; he went thirty, he went all over. He never got caught in that corner again. He just increased his quality of life by oodles. I was so proud of myself. I was so proud of him. That has stuck in my life as one of the best professional things I have ever done. I just feel so privileged to be part of that individual's life and to help him. You just do not get moments like that very often.

Faith's story of contributing to the basic dignity of another person denotes the importance most HSPs place on engaging in meaningful work. HSPs need to feel that their work is meaningful and significant. Faith's willingness to go beyond the prepared plan directly contributed to William's success at learning to self-propel. This is a wonderful example of everyday creativity, passion, and caring for others in deep and meaningful ways.

Olivia's empowered embodiment

People who are oriented to integrating a kind of contemplative, spacious reflective, thoughtful tier of life into a kind of action-oriented society is incredibly necessary. I think that there are many types of people who can contribute that whether they are highly sensitive or not, but I do think that there is something about being sensitive that attunes us to that possibility and to be able to make that mark in the world and to be able to own it or embody it in a confident way and invite people into that, because, I think, ultimately, it is a need to skillfully enact life, you know in our own vivacious way in our community, in our society. I think that is what I often see as an offering that I contributed into all kinds of groups and the more confident and comfortable I am expecting that, the more it is an invitation for others.

This kind of wanting to underscore that tension of the usefulness of the HSP label and getting to know ourselves, but then also not fixating on that. If we only see ourselves through that lens, it is like we can sort of cocoon ourselves more and want to control everything in our lives and so there is a sense of releasing the pressure of it, at the same time being incredibly gentle and caring with myself and knowing who I am and letting that inform how I show up in the world about the work I do. At the same time, the willingness to be surprised and to meet the woman of tomorrow or next week or next month and surprise me in terms of what she is interested in or how she wants to engage the world. Being willing to be in the contradiction and the tension pool generally creates tensions to me is really important.

I would definitely say getting to know oneself is the most important thing and being willing to be surprised just in the sense that, through acknowledging that, I am highly sensitive and introverted. I have also been able to encounter the part of me that is more outgoing or vivacious and that I can play with that and that sometimes my personality can be in contradiction and that it is okay to be in that connection and not creating tension. Self-care is really important. It is kind of like the self-care, getting to know oneself, and then being willing to be surprised. For me, having a very genuine, honest relationship with myself is important. I can feel when I am out of alignment with that and kind of when I have to check in with that and being willing to kind of get to know myself over and over and over again as I change over the years. It is like acknowledging that I am highly sensitive on the one hand was incredibly liberating, but I also do not want to hold it too preciously.

I guess maybe I am also over the fact of the idea. You know, and just sort of see it as this rich field of possibility and that diversity of our contributions are so important. Once I was able to relax into that, it just kind of imparted confidence in my life. I have things set up as a freelancer so that certain pieces of work can grow and shrink over time. What I might be doing for income might change constantly, but I have a real sense of my philosophy and purpose. I also do not really have any problems with self-discipline, and I just love being able to arrange my days based on my needs and how I feel. Autonomy is incredibly important to me. I have a purpose statement about how I oriented my life regularly as part of contemplation and preparing for the day. I have a sense of the path that I am going to be on for my life. What that looks like could change. I know that I have the capacity to range across human expression, human characteristics, and human personality traits. I have set up my life in a way that I can be responsive to little changes and fluctuations. I think it would be much, much harder to be in that place if I did not have the kind of autonomy that I do.

Olivia is an empowered HSP who points out the limiting power of labels. Saying that we are an HSP, and embodiment of what it means to be an HSP, are different things. Olivia has made the efforts to get to know herself and realizes that this knowledge will evolve as she ages. Her emphasis on having a contemplative practice keeps her grounded, calm, and provides an effective self-soothing capability. Olivia also very effectively has set up her life in such a way as to retain ultimate control over her days. Autonomy is an extremely important factor for HSPs.

Kirk's compromise for calling

I worked at ###. I have worked on as a contractor with ### twice. I have worked for multiple other places here in town that you may not have heard of; they were technology places. I worked for the state for a couple of different agencies. I have done contract work for some of those same agencies multiple times. Right now, I am working for the city of ###. That is a contract job as well. I have done about half and half of being a full-time employee and being a contract employee. I find that the contracting situation, even though there is more risk involved it, just feels better to me. I feel more independent. Also, if I can save some money, it allows me to take some breaks between jobs, which has been a life saver for me.

It is important for me, for a couple of reasons. One is, just that if I could go back and kind of redesign some things with some better information, I would have made it a goal early in my life to develop some kind of situation where I could work for myself. Autonomy is very important to me, and I didn't realize how important it was, and I didn't realize that I might have had some options to sort of establish that in a better way when I was younger because I had no guidance and no one to really talk to about these things.

135

The other thing is that I really have never liked what I do for a living. I did it because I was in a situation where I had been exposed to some technology working for ###, even though I was on a factory floor, and I was on my own and I didn't have any help. I had to put myself through school, so I have known since the time I was fifteen or sixteen years old that what I really wanted to do was just write. I did not feel that opportunity would be available to me, so I chose something I thought was pragmatic. That is how I got into technology, but I do not like it. I have never liked it. I almost changed my major, seriously. I spent the first semesters just looking at other majors because I did not like it much all the way through college. What these breaks between contracts do for me is allow me to be away from the stuff that I have to do every day that I don't want to do forever, and it allows me to do some writing and have the time and the space to do that.

That is what I consider to be my real work. That is what I would be doing if I did not have any financial constraints. As I said, I knew when I was fifteen or so that is what I wanted to do, but I did not think it was financially possible to do it. I continue to write. I continue to journal. I spend as much time trying to do that work and cultivate it and get it out as soon as I can. I am frustrated daily because my natural schedule would be to get up in the late morning. My prime time to write is before noon. That is when things come naturally to me. If I do not have that part of the day, it is hard for me to get anything done. That is what I consider to be my work, but the other is my job.

Kirk's story is one of pragmatic consideration (the need to earn a living) mixed with his need for following his true passion (writing). He brought up the point that he did not have guidance early on even though he knew at 15 he wanted to be a writer. Kirk's potential as a writer did not abate, and he did continue to develop through his journaling practice and initial publishing forays. An individual with high developmental potential will develop, whether in supportive or unsupportive conditions. The growth and progress will be much greater in a supportive environment, but Kirk's experience as a writer is likely representative of a number of HSPs, who know they have a focused talent and wish to pursue it, yet are stymied along the way by family responsibilities, financial considerations, or limitations of one's environment. Kirk makes the compromise of doing contract work to provide him with downtime he needs to stay balanced as well as time to work on his writing, which for him is when he thrives.

Seth's insight into the conscientious HSP at work

I think the concept of a highly sensitive person is not recognized in any workplace I have been in, especially on a management level. I think some of the coworkers need to realize you are an introspective and sensitive person, but even my direct manager does not really notice it. He is just confused as to what is going on. He does not know my people disagree with some of his decisions because he is not an introspective person at all. My previous boss was a little more introspective. He was still one of the guys and liked going out drinking kind of stuff, but he was a little more interested in his people than just the position being filled. Whereas my new boss is more interested in what the job title is. One of the things where that really shows is where we got assigned projects. My old boss was good at knowing who was working on a particular part of a program, and he would assign that person, or that person's understudy, an appropriate task. My new boss just kind of throws stuff out there, so I will get something when it should have been assigned to someone beside me who was working on it.

I like a sense of accomplishment and making progress, especially on things that are not trivial or short term. I really do not like, or am not motivated, to do things that are patchwork; something that we know we are going to have to fix in three months. I am not terribly motivated to do this little interim thing. I would rather fix it now, rather than waste the time on this little intermediate thing. I am very goal driven. I am also very quality driven. It is not about quantity, but to turn out a good product that is maintainable and anybody else can look at and know what is going on. I am not one of those people that is into job security through writing bad code that only I can fix. I would rather write something right so anybody can work on it because I get bored with working on the same thing all the time. If I design the code right, I can go on to something else. I do not like doing a new thing every day, but I would rather do one thing a week and move on to something for the next week.

I think employers should view HSPs as an asset, because they tend to be a little less gung-ho about whatever they are doing. Companies are always looking for diversity in the workplace and, right now, diversity means you have a black guy and a female, but what they should be looking for is diversity of ideas in people, and I think they are looking at the wrong metrics, at the moment. If you have the diversity of ideas and thought processes, then you will get those multiple viewpoints you are looking for. The highly sensitive people could give you a little more of that introspective long-term analytical view. The gung-ho people can drag those more introspective people forward at a slightly faster pace, and the

HSP's can hold people in that happy medium where you are making good progress, and you are not going off in one direction all the time.

I think HSP's would be very good in kind of a team lead position where they are leading, directing, a small team, because they are a lot more attuned to how people around them are doing and so they might notice if one of their subordinates is having a tough time earlier than an extravert or somebody who doesn't pay as much attention to that. They also tend to be a lot more detail oriented and analytical than a lot of the people around them. They tend to look at more than one aspect of a problem. Sometimes evaluate two or three solutions to a problem and then figure out which one will have the least impact. I think there is kind of a check to the creative, driven extroverted types.

Seth's insights into the reflective and analytical capabilities of many HSPs offers us a frank glimpse into the struggles many HSPs face in the workplace surrounded by less sensitive, less introspective individuals. Though the HSP is very good at planning, big picture, thinking, and minimizing risk, many employers often choose to go with what is fastest, easiest, and least expensive, often to their chagrin as projects or products require extensive reworking. Seth's role as the empathetic teacher, wise leader, and a conscientious employee is exemplary in that his embodiment of a secure emotionally androgynous male HSP expresses itself with real credibility in a mainstream workplace where sensitivity is not understood or appreciated.

Lucy's yoga journey to authentic work

Following your passion, for me, it was doing what I do easily and not having to work so hard at it. I am using the talents that I never really put to full use; the talents that I had collected over the years. My ability to get people moving forward, my ability to connect and look at the big picture, but also see how to get there. For me, yoga was life changing, so I wanted to keep doing that. Now, when I quit this last year, I do my own private yoga, a lot of professional growth classes for parks and recreation department here, and for some other people, especially highly sensitive people. Helping them find ways to learn who they are and how they can be the best version of themselves. That is my passion.

My friends kept saying, "You need to try yoga, you need to try yoga," because I was being a control freak and not very flexible with my body. I was not anyway. I was like, I do not want to sit still for that, but I think after my first class I was sold on this is what I need, so my husband started going together with me. I would take every class I could, and it was awesome at first, but it was my heart opener. It was me starting to focus inward, instead of trying to be what everybody wanted me to be. That was my first; I call it my heart opener to figuring out who I really was and what I really wanted.

The thing for me, that makes me feel alive, is deep connections with someone. Sometimes, we try too hard to have these connections. After I quit that first job, where for twelve years I had deep connections, it was so hard to walk away from those people, in that place, because the culture was awesome. I did not have that kind of team, at my next place, and they did not appreciate each other's strengths, so instead of trying to bond with those people, I just made it work. I was just like, this is work, and I bonded with the customers that I already bonded with, or family or friends, I just did not even try at that place, if that makes any sense.

So, I just think there is a lot of work to be done on understanding tuning into your own self so you can work with your strengths and understanding how that fits in with everyone around you. That, to me, is the value of what we can explain and calling it a highly sensitive person in the sense that people think you cry all the time or that we are super sensitive to everything. There are those at that end of the spectrum, but those of us who test like extraverted on all of those tests know that it is more about how I process the world. How much information I can get from one scene or one explanation or one movie or one book, you know, on many different levels when you take it in and have different questions you have a different way you are going to remember it. You have a different way that you are going to tell it to someone else. And then, it is about understanding your strengths and working with those, instead of trying to make the weaknesses better.

Lucy's discovery of yoga opened a rich world of inner possibilities for helping other HSPs realize their authentic potential. She has made it her business to intertwine her deep passion for connecting with others to helping them move forward in life. To combine passion with calling is to reach a state of flow or a place where effort seems like play, and one can experience deep engagement of capacities.

Kurt's healing from trauma through performance

I joined the AmeriCorps and basically took a 70% pay cut. I used some of my retirement money just to live, and I basically worked with young people in about five different schools. That kind of catapulted me into working with youth. Something else I did around that time is become a brother in the Big Brothers program. I did that for about five years. That was an amazing experience and opened me to the idea of working with young people. I realized I was very good at working with youth, so it was discovering what I was good at.

In my first year of being in the AmeriCorps, I also was interested in, like I thought I could be in therapy. I was telling my therapist that. My experiences were very dramatic, just in my home. It was always adrenaline filled, and there was always something going on. She recommended that I do something called psychodrama, which was using theater to work through past experiences. That was really an amazing experience. I was working with this group; I think there was me and five other people who were all trained by licensed therapists, and I didn't have a bachelor's yet, but we were doing this work together around family issues. I began to do some healing around some of the chaos that had happened from the trauma. That led into a lot of the work that I am doing now, which is working in schools and kind of facilitation. For five years, I did a one-man performance on the civil rights movement that toured different cities. I initially did a reading for this script, and I had never acted in a scripted piece before. I did a horrible job. I was not reading well, and the director said this was not really the best reading, and I said, "Well, this is my parent's story." This is the civil rights movement that they went through. I want to do this, and so he trained me. He sat with me for two months and trained me to perform this

For five years, I did this and did hundreds of performances. Every time my hands were sweating, I was just completely nervous before the show. It was like I was completely doing it for the first time. It was like it did not come naturally. It felt like something I needed to work through. I was noticing, as I performed, that I did not really like the attention. I did not like being the center, but I was. I had 500 students in an assembly, and they were always great, but it was kind of crazy, so it was not something I wanted to continue.

That was kind of the work that I dove into. I went back to school at a university in Seattle. I liked the idea. There were a few flight attendants who had gone back to get psychology degrees and so I went back, and I liked the fact that you can design your own degree, so I was able to use some of the theater work that I was doing, which was also a lot of social change theater, and actually write about it, and I feel like I really thrived. I feel like I was able to write and really analyze, and, really, a lot of the things that I have been doing for years, but not really validating it. It started coming together in that way.

I do not think I have gotten it completely. I think I am on a good path. I am sincerely hoping to see what happens, because I am still kind of looking at myself and recovering memories and parts of myself, and I am not necessarily actively in therapy right now. Just doing the work that I do, I think it is amazing. What I thought I knew yesterday changes drastically, sometimes within twenty-four hours, but I feel like I am on a good path. I think I am too cautious to say I am there because those things are still in me and a part of who I am. I am on a good journey.

Kurt's story of healing from trauma represents a continuously evolving process of self-therapy in a unique way: through performance. Many HSPs (male and female) never publicly work through their often-hidden inner struggles, but for Kurt, it seems to be cathartic and puts him, as he says, "on a good path." Career for some HSPs may well be interwoven with a healing journey as one seeks to work through healing from past trauma, abuse, neglect, or conflict.

Linda's merging of intellect, creativity, and introspection

In the big picture, I like systems. When I was working in engineering at the auto plant, I started off working in the environmental impact engineering department. That was cool because it was just one department that provided services to the entire facility and it was a large plant. There were a lot of interesting things to see on the plant floor like manufacturing processes and a lot of materials. Since it was all new to me, I was very interested in it. After a while, when it was not so new, I realized that I did not really fit in. There were some other things that didn't really fit with me very well, but just to deal with some of the environmental issues and OSHA and EPA regulations and to be working with the entire plant as a whole was a lot of fun.

If I get into a task, I can spend probably three or four hours at a time without noticing the time, but a lot of what I am doing now, through my new job, I cannot do that for long stretches at a time. I do need to take breaks, so going to the library where I have to pay more attention to, you know taking your computer with you all the time, doesn't work very well for me.

I have a strong sense of ethics. I can only work in environments that conflict with my sense of ethics for a short time. I have managed to work with companies that do conflict with them without realizing it, until I get in there. I have worked for a bunch of evil places. I learned after finding Elaine Aaron's book on HSP's a little over a year ago that everything I was doing in industry was really bad for me, because my work environments were hot, smelly, noisy, and with lots of people around and with interpersonal contacts being a very important part of the work. When I first got into engineering, I thought it was going to be more technical than interpersonal, so all these other things that are overwhelming can be frustrating. I am surprised I lasted as long as I did in that industry.

When I went to work in public health, that is when I got away from the hot, dirty, noisy, smelly environments. The people were much more educated, more reasonable. It was more of a family environment. My strength is creativity so far. I was working at the ##### at the time when physical activity, nutrition, and obesity were becoming big issues in public health, and physical activity was getting into environment research, like it was herb planting, it was transportation and cars, versus walking or biking. I was in a position to, I mean everything was new, so we were trying to lead the field and motivate research at universities. My creativity was encouraged and utilized more there, and that is really the kind of environment I liked.

Some of the organizations want creativity, but they are frightened of it at the same time. Oh yeah, and everywhere I have worked, if they had asked me to be creative, I always reach a point right before I leave where the boss will tell, or a manager will tell me, that they wanted creativity, but not that much. Now I am working independently, and nobody is going to tell me that because I am not working for anybody. But I do not work well by myself. I tend to run in circles by myself. I need other people to structure my environment and my schedule to some extent.

I wish I had known more about sensitivity at an earlier age, because being opportunistic I would just take the jobs that came along first when I needed them. I have been sort of unemployed through the different job changes. In a way, I kind of wish I had known more about it (sensitivity) earlier so I could use it to strategize because I would have done things differently or avoided the industry altogether and done something else. I realized when I was doing consulting work and tried to think about what I could have done differently to make that career (engineering) work better. It probably would have worked better if I were working in civil engineering in a department designing parks or designing roads and drainage systems rather than industry.

I worked for several people who usually knew who they were looking for and understood what they were getting with me, but then they would leave and the people that replaced them did not. A phrase that I just cannot say seriously to a person is "yes, boss; you are always right." I have run into problems with that several times. Part of the problem is that they would be very egotistical and would want people who would be team players and be enthusiastic team players and very sociable and just fit into the group, and I can't do that.

Nowadays employers, especially younger managers in the younger generation, want everybody to be extraverts. I kind of think of it as the way they manage tradeoffs, so the way that religion used to be was that people had interiors that were recognized as having some sort of moral orientation, and there were stances of humility and guilt and conscience that people were expected to go to church and learn about what to do about humility, guilt, and conscience and manage that for themselves and it can be discussed openly among the people. Now that we have more or less gotten rid of people's interiors, instead of knowing a person's interior, I kind of think that society prefers just to deal with extraverts so people can talk a lot and show what might be in their exteriors instead, so it's kind of doing something superficial rather than doing something deep. HSP's, I think, are caught up in all of that to our detriment.

To be deeply sensitive to the environment and being introspective and just feeling deeply about anything is a part of what it is to be highly intelligent, and that has been lost too, because other people try to homogenize the population by saying people should be like the statistical average, and their interior should not be any more than that. Anybody can achieve anything anybody else can if they are working hard enough, and that is not true. That is a bunch of bull shit.

I am also trying to get away from highly detailed, quantitative work, and it is difficult because that is what people want me to do more of, but I think if I can do science and theology then that is going to really push me to my limits of creativity and be very satisfied.

Linda's story of mismatch in a career is typical of many HSPs. No doubt most of us wish we had known much earlier in life about sensory processing sensitivity because we could have more intelligently planned our lives. Her mention of the rich interior of HSPs offers the hope that society will move back from an exterior only stance to one that is more human and perhaps more humane. Linda's experiences as a highly intelligent, professional HSP, articulates a need to thrive as she describes seeking out circumstances that will push her to grow to her full capacities.

Faith's mission of passionate compassion

It is like someone needs to carry me and sometimes cry for the people because that is something that needs to be done. Sometimes I feel that way as an HSP. Sometimes I will just start crying and feeling something so intensely that I feel that is a task maybe all these intense feelings we have whether it is joyous or not, maybe that is why we are here. We are the unique ones to do this. It is not a bad thing. Somebody needs to see the beauty that is here. Somebody needs to cry for those who cannot cry for themselves. Somebody needs to laugh for those who cannot laugh. I know that is mysticism. It is a strange privilege.

It is important for me to make a difference, no matter how small. I have learned, even when I was 20, that all work is meaningful and no matter what it is and, if it isn't apparent, you have to find it, because all work is meaningful. It does really help me to know that I am a part of a greater good, even though it is in a small way. That is extremely important to me, even if I go in the community, and I have done a little thing for somebody and helped them in a small way that is important to me because people have helped me.

Sometimes people have just smiled at me and made me feel better, so I have come to understand what a difference that makes. I am not religious, but I consider myself spiritual. As I get older, I feel like I am becoming wiser and it is really helping me to build my compassionate side and my kindness, and that is something that I am really striving toward.

These days, make sure you take practicality into account because as much as you would like to do something you have to look at the bottom line and sometimes you have to be practical and look at what is going to put a roof over your head and food on the table, rather than what you would ideally like to do. Sometimes, you must take something you would like that is not your ideal job and leave the things you really love for your time off. My job is a good example. I like what I do. I am a medical transcriptionist who specializes in radiology. I am excellent at it. It uses a lot of my skills. It uses all my language skills, my belief in research, it meets a lot of my needs. I enjoy doing it. Is it my ideal job? No, but it is good enough. I wish it paid a little more, but that is the way it is. The things I love to do would not pay me at this point, and I am too old to go back to school. It would not be worth the cost for another ten years. The things that I love to do: my art, my needlework, my digital photography, my singing is stuff I keep for my time off.

One of the things I would tell HSP's is keep your ideals, but be practical as well, because the world is not nice to HSP's. You cannot expose your vulnerabilities too much because this world will eat you alive. Employers do not really give a damn who you are. They want you to do the work and get the job done and they really do not care what you are like. This is not the world it was when I started college in 1976. It is a make sure to keep your ass clear of the sharp pains of the world place. I never used to feel so jaded, but my experiences in the last ten years have taught me otherwise. Nobody cares what you like. It is very much like the army. Having been an army wife, it was very much like that. What employers should do and what employers are doing are completely opposite. It really is against the grain with me. I am lucky right now that I have a fantastic boss. I am extremely glad that I work from home, and we do not have meetings. We do not even have yearly evaluation forms. I love that.

Faith's cautionary insights regarding the demeanor of the corporate mentality are starkly realistic, yet that is the working world we live in, and we should view it as accurately as possible. Faith has found a reasonable compromise in her working life that "pays the bills" and for many people that is enough. It would be counterproductive for me to recommend a grand vision of ultimate work that satisfies our deepest needs. Faith, in a very pragmatic way, has offered us her vision that her work matters, that it helps others (even in a small way) and she is free to pursue her passion for meaning making through other means. Faith is right: being an HSP is a "strange privilege" as we experience surrogate emotions many others ignore or have lost the capacity to feel.

Taylor's creative journey to meaning

I do not want to work in an environment with people that are not kind or not nice. I am too sensitive for that, and I am kind, and I want to be around kind people. I worked at the church and even though I do not attend church, I feel like it is an extension of my community.

I was an interior decorator; an antique dealer; I worked at a construction company in administration; and I was a television producer. Then, I was an executive director at a nonprofit and then finally I am back doing administrative work. I feel like my career has stepped back over twelve years, and that is because of my health. I cannot work 60 hours a week. I cannot, like when you work at a nonprofit, usually, you end up losing jobs and you work a lot more than 40 hours, I just can't do that. I need at least 9 hours of sleep, and I do not sleep very well.

There is a new company in #####, and if I stay in #### there is this conservatory, and I would like to work for the conservatory, because I think it would be magical to work for a circus. I feel like my whole life, all these things that I have been doing, was like a community toolbox.

I got the free speech, democracy, and the advocacy from the TV station. I have the economics from the time bank. Now I feel like, even though I am in an administrative position, I am in a spiritual environment. It is about humanity, so I have this religious piece. The next thing I really want to do has to do with play. I think play is a powerful tool in the toolbox for being healthy. When you are playing, and you are happy in play, you are not at war. You are at peace, and it brings out your creative gifts. It is collaborative. I would like to get into farming, and I have several opportunities for that. My friend has 160 acres in northern ####. Last year, all the crop he grew, he donated it to the time bank. I would just love, I do not want to be the person out there waiting all the time, but I would love to be the community organizer.

I would love to set up an education program where people can learn farming. I really think that we need to take back food from the corporations and the greatest resistance that you can do is to grow a garden. I think food preservation is important. I think maybe either play or farming, some sort of capacity in farming will be the next tool in my tool chest that will help me to work in my community. I know that, whatever I do, it must feel good spiritually, physically, and emotionally and must be a job that I am proud of. I cannot do something that I am not proud of or where I was hurting somebody else.

Every job I have worked at, they have let me create my physical environment, so I have picked out where my office was. I always had to have more windows. I must have quiet space. They have changed doors for me. They let me pick the colors for my office. The church people have, like everything that gives me an aesthetic feeling, been so sweet. They painted my office. They replaced my ceiling. I cannot stress enough how important that has been for me.

I would say in terms of my intuition and my sensitivities, for the most part, I have been very blessed with falling into a job situation. People have recognized my gifts and talents, and they accommodate me more often than not to meet my needs, so that I would stay.

Taylor's story is a bit unusual, and I recognized early on that she was likely a high sensation seeking HSP. The sensation seeking HSPs are approximately 30% of the HSP population and thrive on novelty, new experiences, creative challenge and a certain amount of disinhibition and possibly thrill seeking. Clearly, Taylor's employers recognized her capacities as unique and were willing to meet her needs to keep her services. Her presentation as an extravert creates enthusiasm in others and perhaps made her ability to fit in somewhat easier because extraversion is the dominant societal personality trait.

Hailey's anxiety, plea for respect, and protective instinct

I have never told anybody, that I am an HSP, because it sounds like some kind of mental disorder. I do not want them to think that because it is taboo in this country, even now. HSPs need to be treated with respect like anybody else. I don't want to say gingerly, because that would refer back to them having a mental illness, but supervisors really need to prepare them well for change, and they need to be available to ask questions of and not be treated like they are weak. They may be overstimulated already, and a supervisor is treating them negatively like "you should already know this," or "that can't happen!" If that HSP comes up to a boss and asks, "can you help and show me how to do something?" that boss should say "absolutely, no problem," and treat them like a human being.

I was very motivated and very devoted; so devoted that I got overstimulated. What motivates me, is the knowledge that I am doing a good job, and I am devoted, and I am conscientious and that I have a strong knowledge base of what I am doing. I have a strong knowledge base of this one client that I am taking care of, and I have a strong knowledge base of a lot of different things.

I think HSPs, when they find the right careers, are the most conscientious, the most devoted people you'll get if they can find where they are happy, because it's very hard for them to go on and look for other jobs and careers. If I find somewhere that I am happy at, which is very hard to do, I will do everything I can to hang onto that.

I would love to do what I'm doing the rest of my life, but I know that cannot happen because this patient isn't going to live forever and I could end up in other homes where I hate it again, but I always have my bachelor's degree, and I'm not even utilizing it and I don't even know, maybe I'd be okay in another situation, but I'm afraid to give myself a chance. The risk of being something I have been in the past, it is not worth it. It is not important enough to be worth the anxiety.

Variety can be scary. Variety for a nurse means you are going to go back into the hospitals and get this person that is that sick and that person that is this sick. To me, it is all negative. So, in nursing anyway, I do not like variety. I think working in the school district was successful, because I was around people, I was around coworkers, I was calm, and I had my own space. When you are a school nurse, you are on your own. I did not have a boss, at least at this particular school, did not have an RN over me. I was making my own decisions, and I was taking care of children who could talk back to me, unlike now where it is all one sided. Although, I feel very fulfilled in that.

As part of the normal working world, the school district

was probably the best place for me. As far as being around other people, being around people with medical issues, parents who needed help; that was the most normal job I have had. It was work in the daytime, I was able to be with my kids in the evening, that worked out well.

I like to work with people who treat each other with respect and who are very smart, but, at the same time, if there is a young nurse who needs help, I like to stay and help them. I like to help them be the best nurse they can be. I believe in hands-on teaching, more than just giving an explanation, because I go back in time when I was a young nurse and people tried to explain things early on showing me and thinking how nervous and overstimulated I was because I didn't get good training in the hospitals and nursing homes. I even had mean people who treated me like I was stupid. I do not want other nurses to go through what I went through and have to be stimulated in the wrong way. I protect them, and I feel like I am protecting them. I have had nurses tell me repeatedly "thank you for being so nice to me."

What I do not like are authoritarian or cocky trainers with a new nurse. *Eating your young* is the worst thing you can do in a career field, especially with me, because I was so sensitive to everything.

Hailey's dedication and conscientiousness have alternately served her well (in establishing her as competent and reliable) but worked against her tendencies for overstimulation and anxiety. She seems to have found a niche in nursing in pediatric home care that works for her because the strong interpersonal component has been lessened. Hailey is able to devote her attention to just one patient and bring her strong empathy and dedication to bear for her patient and for younger nurses who are able to reap the benefits of her negative experiences with her trainers. HSPs often make excellent teachers, trainers, and caregivers (at all levels).

Conclusion

The narratives in this chapter demonstrate the depth of feeling and passion to which HSPs devote themselves in their working lives. From caring professions where empathy is invaluable, to designing programming code where conscientious planning is key to sustainable, low-cost business practices, HSPs function at all levels of society and in all career fields. One of the aspects that I found particularly encouraging was how HSPs from unsupportive, chaotic, even abusive or neglectful childhoods were able to overcome their trauma and pain and externalize their emotions to help others as they heal. As the old saying goes "there's no substitute for experience," and that is no truer than in careers where many of us have suffered and overcome tremendous personal obstacles to become the thriving individuals we are.

For those who are beginning on the road to self-awareness as an HSP or are still in the process at some point, the above narratives represent real-life struggles and triumphs of fellow HSPs. Some have done very well, while others move from position to position in search of one that will work given their unique needs. We are all different, even though we are all highly sensitive people. The only real binding thread is that we all possess the personality trait, sensory processing sensitivity, and that we are all in the process of attempting to act out our being in a fairly hostile societal environment

Thrive

<u>Conclusion</u>

Thrive!

Sensory processing sensitivity is a personality trait that likely evolved because it provided the species with a survival advantage. SPS is a survival trait that must have provided an advantage, on the average, in our ancient past. Individuals in that period who were capable of big picture thinking, high empathy, and careful, innovative planning, and who were able to notice subtleties others missed, must have helped enable the survival of human tribes or SPS would have disappeared from the genes of subsequent generations. It is only in our contrived, largely artificial world where notions of normalcy are decided by corporate usefulness and narrow, arbitrary societal standards of behavior that many HSPs find themselves lost and struggling with capacities less desired by a split community that is more diffused and less intimate.

Our job here has been to explore together the complex activity that is work and career, delve deep into the experiences of HSPs at work, and finally to arrive at pragmatic, practical advice that will enable others to make informed choices regarding career. We have spared no emotions in examining the good, the bad, and the ugly as described by HSPs in both studies. We have investigated the value of empathy and learned how it is also the most significant issue HSPs express as problematic. We have followed that up with a look at how our childhoods have lingering positive and negative effects. We established that even for those who suffered in childhood the effects may largely be overcome in adulthood, though not without serious efforts.

Moving forward, we looked at the importance of self-care, and raised its prominence in our lives to the very highest level. Indeed, we learned self-care must become a spiritual practice, in and of itself, if we are to weather the ups and downs of daily life in the workplace. Next, we probed the inner depths of HSPs and explored the sensory world where so many feel overstimulated; the rich inner world where complexity is prized; and where creativity abides deep in the heart of HSPs. We followed that with the intersection of a separate personality trait, where sensation seeking is complicated by a counterbalancing cautionary sensitivity. We again emphasized the importance of self-care, as sensation seeking HSPs often burn out the sensitive side. Moving to a macro scale, we unraveled the sociological context, within which we all live, and revealed a web of complexity, each segment of which deeply impacts all our lives, the largest of which is gender.

Shifting gears to part three of this book, we explored the results from a large survey and learned much about the types of careers HSPs are already in. We surveyed the rise of virtual home workers and segued into a discussion of self-employment and the trades. Lastly, we allowed HSPs to speak for themselves and offer us their stories of compassion, struggle, triumph, and healing. Now, here we are at the end of this journey, yet, the journey will always continue because we will always have a need for further explorations and insights as we navigate the complicated waters of work and career. After all of this, what is it I am advocating to you as an HSP in search of the right career?

A Robust Embodiment

What does it mean to robustly embody sensory processing sensitivity? What it means is, we become empowered HSPs if we are not; we decisively choose careers that work for us; we manage our need for self-care with attention and sincerity; we embrace masculine and feminine sides of ourselves and live as whole, complete beings with strength and power; we learn resilience and compassion, both for ourselves as well as others; and we accept ourselves quirks and all! After all, being highly sensitive is who we are and how we live. A full 75% of HSPs, in my survey, agreed with the statement, "being a highly sensitive person has been the dominant theme in my life." We acknowledge the role of sensory processing sensitivity in our lives but are not bound by it.

To be an HSP, means we live in a world where we are a large minority, but a minority, nonetheless, and we will experience our share of puzzled looks as we withdraw from interactions others revel in, be told we need to "toughen up," and know we are in very real ways, different. I intentionally avoid overly romanticizing our potential because it simply is not possible for me to speak to over a billion individuals as if we are all the same. Instead, I offer a more pragmatic invitation that accepts us as we are and that offers a thoughtful consideration of the possibilities inherent in our trait.

Highly sensitive people differ from each other in a hundred ways. Some may not even resemble HSPs at all, but their sensitivity marks them as such. Diversity is our strength as HSPs. We offer tremendous capacities for empathy, creativity, and compassion to a world seemingly deluded and ignorant of the value of diversity. Whether we are accepted by society or not, we each have a duty to ourselves and our families to develop our considerable potentials in ways appropriate for each of us. In doing so, we strengthen ourselves, our families, our communities, and, by extension, the world, because culture is constantly being renegotiated by each of us, based on our choices and attitudes.

Thrive!

The changing nature of the workplace means there will be declining opportunities for some and new, emerging opportunities for others. As intuitive individuals with a deep capacity for creativity, empathy, and reflection we should involve ourselves in occupations that take advantage of opportunities for working from home; accept employment with employers who are more in touch with meeting the needs and desires of 21st century workers for greater autonomy and freedom; and develop skills and networks of contacts that will position us to carefully construct the lives we need and want to live.

It is true that HSPs live more complex, complicated lives with emotions serving as a trigger point, but we should always move forward from a strengths perspective emphasizing the ways our myriad of talents and capabilities enhance rather than detract; increase efficiencies through our careful planning and conscientious attention to detail; and serve as emotional barometers, reflecting the way our built and interpersonal working environments affect all of us.

The changes many companies have already put in place are due as much as a response to the need to recruit talent, by offering them the working environment they perceive as desirable, as a need to increase profits. Leading the way, one cannot help but imagine that HSPs have influenced not only employers, but also the next generation of younger workers (our children) who seek the types of conditions they know we value: autonomy, greater freedom to work when and where we wish, and to do interesting meaningful work. Indeed, HSPs seem to be positioned in the new economy in a way that is quite advantageous if we, both, realize what may be available to us and prepare ourselves to take advantage of the possibilities.

It is inevitable that some HSPs will be in a better position to embrace 21st Century opportunities. Many HSPs still face the uphill struggle of overcoming unsupportive, traumatic, or abusive childhoods. Some have given up the struggle and resigned themselves to work that may be stable, but ill-suited to their actual needs. Others may have completely given up altogether and found work, other than paying work; that can satisfy their needs. In both cases, it is at least advisable to develop oneself, outside of work, in activities that provide fulfillment and satisfaction. For those HSPs who can overcome inherently limiting issues, or who come from supportive, nurturing backgrounds the possibilities for creating HSP-friendly lifestyles are increasing in the coming decade.

This book can only hope to begin the discussion of HSPs and careers, because the workplace transformations are ongoing and apply to each person in a specific way. I suggest that interested HSPs keep an eye on emerging trends in the workforce and look for those opportunities that seem to hold promise for fulfilling their needs and not be afraid to make the changes necessary to live full and substantive lives. Before we can thrive, we must learn to survive. Once we have settled on appropriate, sustainable ways that enable our survival we can begin to move from surface level skimming to deeper, more meaningful ways of being that hold the potential for thriving as individuals and communities.

To thrive implies that we have adapted well to survival and are able to flourish. Compared to a survival mode, where our focus is immediate, singular, and narrowly focused, thrive mode is connective, broad, plural, and inclusive of present and future considerations and possibilities. Thriving, however, is not, and does not, look the same for every HSP. Just as we are somewhat different in how our lived experiences have affected who we are, so to the definition of thriving for each HSP will be different. To thrive does not mean we find ourselves in a constant state of flow or peak experiences. Indeed, life does have its routine, even dull periods for all of us. What thrive does imply is that, overall, we have such a collection of engaged, positive, challenging growth-oriented experiences throughout life that we can consider our lives to have been fruitful, worthwhile, and well-lived. Just as the flowers of summer require careful watering, feeding, and pruning, we HSPs must tend ourselves to reap the harvest of rich possibilities, inherent in us all.

Key takeaways from this book

•   Empathy is a double-edged sword that simultaneously enables you to enter another person's experience, while also predisposing you toward an extreme sensitivity toward negative, arrogant, or manipulative individuals. Learn to say no, set boundaries without apology, and limit your exposure to individuals who are draining.

•   Childhood trauma, abuse, and neglect do not need to be limiting and may be mitigated or overcome in large part through our own efforts or with the help of skilled counseling. Our choices as adults do not need to mirror those of anyone else.

• Self-care is more than just a buzzword it must be a spiritual practice for HSPs. Self-care should include physical, emotional, social, and spiritual dimensions including the development of a contemplative practice.

• HSPs are perfectly fine the way we are! We do not need to "toughen up," "take things less seriously," or "get a thicker skin." It's the rest of the population that needs to work on their compassion, empathy, simple kindness, and appreciate that some people exist to keep us fully "human." Revel in your beautiful quietude and deep, soulful mind! Be joyous in your differentness!

• HSPs are not limited in choice of careers. Choices should be based on unique individual needs and preferences. All careers are open to HSPs!

• Work is changing, and HSPs may be uniquely well-positioned to take advantage of home and on-demand work arrangements.

• Self-employment may be a viable alternative to traditional employment but proceed with caution and do your research first.

• You are not the only one struggling to find the right career!

Above all else, work out ways that sustainably and reasonably allow you to survive, so that you may THRIVE!

Invictus

Out of the night that covers me,
Black as the pit from pole to pole,
I thank whatever gods may be
For my unconquerable soul.

In the fell clutch of circumstance
I have not winced nor cried aloud.
Under the bludgeoning's of chance
My head is bloody, but unbowed.

Beyond this place of wrath and tears
Looms but the Horror of the shade,
And yet the menace of the years
Finds and shall find me unafraid.

It matters not how strait the gate,
How charged with punishments the scroll,
I am the master of my fate,
I am the captain of my soul.

William Ernest Henley

Chapter 1

Elaine Aron & Arthur Aron. "Sensory processing sensitivity and its relation to introversion and emotionality." *Journal of Personality and Social Psychology, 73*, (1997), 352.

[2] Barron, F. (1995). *No rootless flower.* Cresskill, NJ: Hampton Press.

[3] Frankl, V. (1984). *Man's search for meaning.* New York, NY: Simon and Schuster, Inc.

[4] Cooper. T. (2014). *"The integral being: A qualitative investigation of highly sensitive persons and temperament-appropriate careers."* ProQuest/UMI Dissertation Publishing, Ann Arbor

Chapter 2

Heerwagen, J., Heerwagen, J.H., Kelly, K., & Kampschroer, K. (2010). The changing nature of organizations, work, and workplace. U.S. General Services Administration.

[2] Csikszentmihalyi, M. (1992a). *Flow: The psychology of happiness.* London: Harper and Row.
Csikszentmihalyi, M. (1996). *Creativity: Flow and the psychology of discovery and invention.* New York, NY: HarperCollins Publisher.
Csikszentmihalyi, M. (1993). *"The evolving self: A psychology for the third millennium."* New York, NY: HarperCollins Publisher.

[3] Bernstein, E. (2015). *"Do you cry easily? You may be a highly sensitive person."* Wall Street Journal. May 18.

Chapter 3

Acevedo, B., Aron, A., Aron, E., Sangster, M., Collins, N., & Brown, L. (2014). The highly sensitive brain: An fMRI study of sensory processing sensitivity and response to others' emotions. *Brain and Behavior, 4*, 1-15.
Aron, A., Aron., E., & Jagiellowicz, J. (2012). Sensory processing sensitivity: A review in the light of the evolution of biological responsivity. *Personality and Social Psychology Review, 16*, 262-282.

Aron, E., Aron, A., & Davies, K. (2005). Adult shyness: The interaction of temperamental sensitivity and an adverse childhood environment. *Personality and Social Psychology Bulletin, 31*, 181-197.

[2] Zeff, T. (2010). *The strong sensitive boy*. San Ramon, CA: Prana Publishing.

[3] Jung, C. (1921). *Psychological types*. Collected Works, Vol. 6. Princeton, NJ: The Princeton University Press.

[4] Judge, T., Higgins, C., Thoresen, C., & Barrick, M. (1999). The big five personality traits, general mental ability, and career success across the life span. *Personnel Psychology, 52*(3), 621-652.

Chapter 4
  Aron, E. (2010). *Psychotherapy and the highly sensitive person: Improving outcomes for that minority of people who are the majority of clients*. New York, NY: Routledge.

  Aron, A., Aron., E., & Jagiellowicz, J. (2012). Sensory processing sensitivity: A review in the light of the evolution of biological responsivity. *Personality and Social Psychology Review, 16*, 262-282.

[2] Aron, A., & Aron, E. (1997). Sensory-processing sensitivity and its relation to introversion and emotionality. *Journal of Personality and Social Psychology, 73*, 345-368.

[3] Csikszentmihalyi, M. (1996). *Creativity: Flow and the psychology of discovery and invention*. New York, NY: HarperCollins Publisher.

[4] Storr, A. (1993). *The dynamics of creativity*. New York, NY: Random House.

[5] Overview of learning styles. Retrieved from http://www.learning-styles-online.com/overview.

Chapter 5
  Zuckerman, M. (1979). *Sensation seeking: Beyond the optimal level of arousal*. Hillsdale, NJ: Lawrence Erlbaum Associates.
  Zuckerman, M. (1983). *Biological bases of sensation seeking, impulsivity and anxiety*. Hillsdale, NJ: Lawrence Erlbaum Associates.

[2] Zuckerman, M., 2007. *Sensation seeking and risky behavior*. Washington, DC:

American Psychological Association.

[3] Jaeger, B. (2004). *Making work work for the highly sensitive person*. New York, NY: McGraw-Hill.

[4] Aron, E. (2000). *The highly sensitive person in love*. New York, NY: Broadway Books.

Chapter 6
Mills, C. (1959). *The sociological imagination*. New York, NY: Oxford University Press.

[2] Morin, E. (2001). *"Seven complex lessons in education for the future."* UNESCO Publishing.

[3] Henslin, J. (2013). *"Essential of sociology."* New York, NY: Pearson.

[4] Bowles, S., & Gintis, H. (1976). *Schooling in capitalistic America*. New York, NY: Basic Books.
Bowles, S., & Gintis, H. (2002). Schooling in capitalistic America revisited. *Sociology of Education, 75*, 1-18.

[5] Marx, K., and Engles, F. (1967). *Communist manifesto*. New York, NY: Pantheon.

[6] Knapp, P. (1994). *One World – Many Worlds: Contemporary Sociological Theory* (2nd Ed.). HarperCollins College Div, pp. 228–246.

Chapter 7
Csikszentmihalyi, M. (1993). *"The evolving self: A psychology for the third millennium."* New York, NY: HarperCollins Publisher.

[2] Schadler, T., Brown, M., & Burnes, S. (2009). "U.S. telecommuting forecast, 2009-2016: A digital home report." Retrieved from https://www.forrester.com/US+Telecommuting+Forecast+2009+To+2016/fulltext/-/E-RES46635?objectid=RES46635.

[3] Koloc. N. (2014). "Let employees choose when where and how to work." Retrieved from https://hbr.org/2014/11/let-employees-choose-when-where-and-how-to-work.

[4] Graber, S. (2105). "Why remote work thrives in some companies and fails in others." Retrieved from https://hbr.org/2015/03/why-remote-work-thrives-in-some-companies-and-fails-in-others

[5] Bloom, N., & Roberts, J. (2015). "A working from home experiment shows high performers like it better." Retrieved from https://hbr.org/2015/01/a-working-from-home-experiment-shows-high-performers-like-it-better.

[6] SBA advice available from https://www.sba.gov/tools/local-assistance/sbdc.

Chapter 8
Seligman, M. (2006). *Learned optimism: How to change your mind and your life*. New York, NY: Random House.

About the Author

Tracy Cooper, Ph.D., received his Doctor of Philosophy in Integral Studies (personality psychology focus) from the California Institute of Integral Studies in San Francisco, CA. He appeared in the documentary movie *Sensitive – The Untold Story* with many other researchers who are actively exploring the personality trait Sensory Processing Sensitivity. His expertise on HSPs and careers has led him to practice one on one consulting with HSPs in career crisis or transition. He currently leads a Master of Liberal Arts degree as Program Chairman at Baker University, founded Invictus Publishing, llc, and continues to conduct new research, most recently into the high sensation seeking highly sensitive person. He lives in the Springfield, Missouri metro area with his wife, Lisa, and son, Ben. His blog may be found at his web site: www.drtracycooper.wordpress.com, and his Facebook page may be found at @tracycooperphd.

Made in United States
Troutdale, OR
01/04/2025

27603450R00121